COOKING WITH HERBS & SPICES

COOKING WITH HERBS & SPICES

Rosemary Jones

LANGHAM PRESS

Contents

Notes

Standard spoon measurements are used in all recipes
1 tablespoon = one 15 ml spoon
1 teaspoon = one 5 ml spoon
All spoon measures are level

For all recipes, quantities are given in metric, imperial and American measures. Follow one set of measures only because they are not interchangeable. Ovens and grills (broilers) should be preheated to specified temperature or heat setting.

First published 1983 by Langham Press, Langham Park, Catteshall Lane, Godalming, Surrey

In association with Octopus Books Limited, 59 Grosvenor Street, London, W1

ISBN 0 86362 014 0

Produced by Mandarin Publishers Limited
22a Westlands Road, Quarry Bay, Hong Kong

Printed in Hong Kong

Introduction

From earliest times, herbs and spices have been used to add flavour and interest to food, as well as for their medicinal properties. In medieval times, every large house or monastery would have a herb garden to supply the needs of their communities. Nowadays, it is quite possible to grow most herbs in pots on a sunny patio, balcony or even a window-sill, to provide for the needs of today's smaller households. And it is well worth growing your own fresh herbs; seeds or young plants are inexpensive, and the taste of fresh herbs is much superior to the taste of dried herbs, which can add a dry, musty flavour to food. If you do use dried herbs, remember that drying intensifies their flavour, and use about half as much as you would of the fresh herb.

Once picked, fresh herbs can be kept for a day or two in a jug of water. Alternatively, they can be stored in a covered plastic box in the refrigerator. Many of the leafy herbs can also be frozen successfully. Wash and dry them well, taking care not to bruise the leaves, then pack them in small amounts in plastic bags or freezer-proof containers. Small quantities of the frozen herb can then be added straight to the dish as it cooks, and will thaw almost immediately.

Spices, of course, have to be bought, and it is well worth finding a supplier whose stock is frequently replenished. Spices lose their pungency if stored for too long, so buy them in as small quantities as possible and replace them if they are stale.

The recipes in this book give many exciting ideas for using herbs and spices, but of course the possibilities are unlimited. A garnish of chopped herbs will enliven any plain dish, or you can make herb butters or salad dressings. Try marinating bland meat such as chicken in different mixtures of spices before casseroling it, or roasting meat with fresh herbs either as stuffing or scattered over before cooking. Fish, too, benefits from the addition of herbs or spices. A typical Mediterranean way of cooking fish or meat is to grill it over an open fire of dried fennel stalks, and you can experiment with other herbs such as rosemary or thyme, if you have a barbecue. The pungent smoke from the burning herbs flavours the food, and you can add extra flavour by brushing it as it cooks with a marinade or oil, using a bunch of fresh herbs as a brush.

Using this book as your guide, experiment with different combinations of taste and texture and discover new possibilities for using herbs and spices in everyday as well as elaborate dishes, to make your cooking more imaginative and delicious.

Soups & Starters

Lovage Soup

METRIC/IMPERIAL	AMERICAN
25 g/1 oz butter	*2 tablespoons butter*
1 onion, peeled and roughly chopped	*1 onion, peeled and roughly chopped*
1 kg/2 lb freshly picked lovage	*2 lb freshly picked lovage*
1.2 litres/2 pints well-flavoured chicken stock	*5 cups well-flavoured chicken stock*
salt	*salt*
freshly ground pepper	*freshly ground pepper*
2 eggs	*2 eggs*
2 × 15 ml spoons/2 tablespoons freshly grated Parmesan cheese	*2 tablespoons freshly grated Parmesan cheese*
2 × 15 ml spoons/1 tablespoon chopped fresh parsley	*1 tablespoon chopped fresh parsley*

Heat the butter in a pan and cook the onion for 5 minutes without browning. Stir in the lovage and stock and season with salt and pepper. Bring to the boil and simmer for 10 minutes. Purée the soup in a blender or food processor or rub through a sieve (strainer). Return the soup to the pan and bring to the boil. Mix together the eggs, Parmesan cheese and parsley. Remove the soup from the heat and stir in the egg mixture. Ladle into warmed serving dishes.

SERVES 4 TO 6

Mushroom and Sherry Soup

METRIC/IMPERIAL	AMERICAN
25 g/1 oz butter	*2 tablespoons butter*
1 onion, peeled and chopped	*1 onion, peeled and chopped*
225 g/8 oz button mushrooms, thinly sliced	*2 cups button mushrooms, thinly sliced*
900 ml/1½ pints chicken or vegetable stock	*3¾ cups chicken or vegetable stock*
1 × 5 ml spoon/1 teaspoon lemon juice	*1 teaspoon lemon juice*
1 × 5 ml spoon/1 teaspoon fresh thyme, or 1 × 2.5 ml spoon/½ teaspoon dried thyme	*1 teaspoon fresh thyme, or ½ teaspoon dried thyme*
salt	*salt*
freshly ground black pepper	*freshly ground black pepper*
2 × 15 ml spoons/2 tablespoons sherry (dry or medium)	*2 tablespoons sherry (dry or cream)*
2 × 15 ml spoons/2 tablespoons chopped fresh parsley or thyme to garnish	*2 tablespoons chopped fresh parsley or thyme to garnish*

Heat the butter in a saucepan and fry the onion for 5 minutes until lightly browned. Add the mushrooms and fry for 2 minutes. Pour in the stock and add the lemon juice, thyme, salt and pepper. Bring to the boil and simmer for 5 minutes. Stir in the sherry. Serve hot, sprinkled with parsley or thyme.

SERVES 6

Gazpacho

METRIC/IMPERIAL	AMERICAN
1 large onion, peeled and chopped	*1 large onion, peeled and chopped*
1 cucumber, peeled and chopped	*1 cucumber, peeled and chopped*
1 green pepper, cored, seeded and chopped	*1 green pepper, seeded and chopped*
1 clove garlic, chopped	*1 clove garlic, chopped*
450 g/1 lb tomatoes, peeled, seeded and chopped	*2 cups peeled, seeded and chopped tomatoes*
1 × 15 ml spoon/1 tablespoon chopped fresh parsley	*1 tablespoon chopped fresh parsley*
1 × 15 ml spoon/1 tablespoon chopped fresh mint	*1 tablespoon chopped fresh mint*
few almonds or hazelnuts (optional)	*few almonds or hazelnuts (optional)*
1 × 15 ml spoon/1 tablespoon olive oil	*1 tablespoon olive oil*
1 × 15 ml spoon/1 tablespoon wine vinegar	*1 tablespoon wine vinegar*
1 × 2.5 ml spoon/½ teaspoon salt	*½ teaspoon salt*
white pepper to taste	*white pepper to taste*
1 litre/1¾ pints water	*4¼ cups water*
To garnish:	To garnish:
1 onion, peeled and finely diced	*1 onion, peeled and finely diced*
¼ cucumber, peeled and finely diced	*¼ cucumber, peeled and finely diced*
1 red or green pepper, cored, seeded and finely diced	*1 red or green pepper, seeded and finely diced*
12 olives, stoned and sliced	*12 pitted olives, sliced*

Put all the ingredients, except the water, into a blender or food processor and blend at the lowest speed for about 1 minute or until smooth. Alternatively, pound these ingredients together, using a pestle and mortar. Pour into a large serving bowl and stir in the water. Cover and chill for several hours before serving. When ready to serve, ice cubes may be added. Serve the garnish ingredients separately in small bowls.

SERVES 4

Gazpacho

Crème Vichyssoise à la Ritz

METRIC/IMPERIAL
60 g/2 oz butter
3 leeks, trimmed, halved and finely sliced
salt
freshly ground white pepper
3 medium potatoes, peeled and diced
1 litre/$1\frac{3}{4}$ pints chicken stock
pinch cayenne
450 ml/$\frac{3}{4}$ pint tomato juice
250 ml/8 fl oz cream
1 teaspoon snipped chives

AMERICAN
$\frac{1}{4}$ cup butter
3 leeks, trimmed, halved and finely sliced
salt
freshly ground white pepper
3 medium potatoes, peeled and diced
4 cups chicken stock
pinch cayenne
2 cups tomato juice
1 cup cream
1 teaspoon chopped chives

Melt the butter in a heavy saucepan, add the leeks and cook over a low heat until soft but not brown, stirring constantly. Season with a little salt and pepper and add the potatoes. Stir in chicken stock and cayenne, cover and simmer for 30 minutes or until the potatoes are tender. Allow to cool. Purée in a blender or food processor fitted with a steel blade, or rub through a sieve (strainer). Stir in the tomato juice and half the cream and chill. Taste for seasoning, spoon into bowls and swirl in a little of the remaining cream on top. Sprinkle with chives.

SERVES 6

Spinach Soup

METRIC/IMPERIAL
450 g/1 lb fresh spinach or 225 g/8 oz packet frozen, chopped spinach, thawed
40 g/1½ oz butter or margarine
1 onion, peeled and chopped
25 g/1 oz plain flour
600 ml/1 pint stock (white, chicken or vegetable)
150 ml/¼ pint milk
grated rind ½ lemon
2 × 5 ml spoons/2 teaspoons lemon juice
1 × 2.5 ml spoon/½ teaspoon grated nutmeg
1 × 1.25 ml spoon/¼ teaspoon grated root ginger
salt
freshly ground black pepper
150 ml/¼ pint single cream
croûtons to garnish

AMERICAN
1 lb fresh spinach, or ½ lb package frozen, chopped spinach, thawed
3 tablespoons butter or margarine
1 onion, peeled and chopped
¼ cup all-purpose flour
2½ cups stock (white, chicken or vegetable)
⅔ cup milk
grated rind ½ lemon
2 teaspoons lemon juice
½ teaspoon grated nutmeg
¼ teaspoon grated ginger root
salt
freshly ground black pepper
⅔ cup light cream
croûtons to garnish

If using fresh spinach, wash it and place it in a saucepan with only the water that clings to it. Cover the pan and cook gently for about 10 minutes until tender. Drain the spinach, squeezing out all the water with a wooden spoon, then chop it finely.

Melt the butter or margarine in a saucepan and fry the onion gently for 5 minutes without browning. Stir in the flour, then add the stock and the milk. Bring to the boil, stirring all the time until the sauce thickens. Stir in the chopped spinach with the lemon rind and juice, nutmeg, ginger, and salt and pepper to taste. Simmer for 5 minutes. For a smoother and greener soup, purée the mixture in a blender or food processor or rub through a sieve. Return the soup to the pan. Stir in most of the cream and reheat without boiling. Serve hot garnished with a swirl of cream and croûtons.
SERVES 6

Persian Noodle Soup

METRIC/IMPERIAL
Meatballs:
225 g/8 oz finely minced beef
1 small onion, grated
1 × 1.25 ml spoon/¼ teaspoon ground cinnamon
1 × 1.25 ml spoon/¼ teaspoon freshly ground black pepper
1 × 2.5 ml spoon/½ teaspoon salt
Soup:
1.2 litres/2 pints water
1.5 × 5 ml spoons/1½ teaspoons salt
50 g/2 oz black-eyed peas
50 g/2 oz lentils
125 g/4 oz fine noodles
1 × 2.5 ml spoon/½ teaspoon freshly ground pepper
4 × 15 ml spoons/4 tablespoons chopped parsley
Spicing:
2 × 15 ml spoons/2 tablespoons chopped fresh mint, or 1 × 15 ml spoons/1 tablespoon dried mint
1 × 2.5 ml spoon/½ teaspoon ground cinnamon
1 × 2.5 ml spoon/½ teaspoon freshly ground pepper

AMERICAN
Meatballs:
1 cup finely ground beef, firmly packed
1 small onion, grated
¼ teaspoon ground cinnamon
¼ teaspoon freshly ground black pepper
½ teaspoon salt
Soup:
2 pints water
1½ teaspoons salt
¼ cup black-eyed peas
¼ cup lentils
¼ cup fine noodles
½ teaspoon freshly ground black pepper
½ cup chopped parsley
Spicing:
2 tablespoons chopped fresh mint, or 1 tablespoon dried mint
½ teaspoon ground cinnamon
½ teaspoon freshly ground pepper

Mix the meatball ingredients thoroughly with your hands until they form a paste, then mould into walnut-size balls and set aside. Put water, salt and black-eyed peas in a large saucepan and simmer for 15 minutes. Add meatballs, lentils, noodles, pepper and parsley and simmer for 15 minutes, or until lentils and peas are tender. Combine mint, cinnamon and pepper and stir into the soup just before removing it from the heat. Serve immediately.
SERVES 6

Fish Chowder

METRIC/IMPERIAL
1 × 15 ml spoon/1 tablespoon oil
2 rashers streaky bacon, rinded and chopped
1 onion, peeled and chopped
1 clove garlic, crushed (optional)
1 celery stick, sliced
1 small green pepper, cored, seeded and chopped
600 ml/1 pint fish stock, strained
1 × 5 ml spoon/1 teaspoon fennel seeds
grated rind ½ lemon
2 × 5 ml spoons/2 teaspoons lemon juice
225 g/8 oz potatoes, peeled and diced
225 g/8 oz firm white fish fillets, skinned (e.g. cod, haddock, coley)
1 bay leaf
150 ml/¼ pint milk
2 × 15 ml spoons/2 tablespoons chopped fresh parsley
salt
freshly ground black pepper

AMERICAN
1 tablespoon oil
2 slices streaky bacon, rinded and chopped
1 onion, peeled and chopped
1 clove garlic, crushed (optional)
1 stalk celery, sliced
1 small green pepper, seeded and chopped
2½ cups fish stock, strained
1 teaspoon fennel seeds
grated rind ½ lemon
2 teaspoons lemon juice
1⅓ cups potatoes, peeled and diced
8 oz firm white fish fillets, skinned (e.g. cod, haddock, coley)
1 bay leaf
⅔ cup milk
2 tablespoons chopped fresh parsley
salt
freshly ground black pepper

Heat the oil in a large saucepan and fry the bacon, onion, garlic, celery and pepper for 5 minutes, without browning. Pour in the stock and stir in the fennel, lemon rind and juice. Add the diced potatoes and bring to the boil. Place the fish on top, in 1 or 2 pieces, with the bay leaf. Cover and simmer for 20 minutes. Remove the bay leaf, stir in the milk and chopped parsley. Reheat, taste and adjust the seasoning.
SERVES 6

Fish Chowder

Goulash Dumpling Soup

METRIC/IMPERIAL	AMERICAN
2 × 15 ml spoons/2 tablespoons oil	*2 tablespoons oil*
50 g/2 oz streaky bacon, rinded and chopped	*3 slices streaky bacon, rinded and chopped*
1 large onion, peeled and chopped	*1 large onion, peeled and chopped*
1 clove garlic, crushed (optional)	*1 clove garlic, crushed (optional)*
2 celery sticks, sliced	*2 stalks celery, sliced*
2 carrots, peeled and sliced	*2 carrots, peeled and sliced*
50 g/2 oz mushrooms, sliced	*½ cup mushrooms, sliced*
1 small green pepper, seeded and sliced	*1 small green pepper, seeded and sliced*
1 × 15 ml spoon/1 tablespoon paprika	*1 tablespoon paprika*
1 × 15 ml spoon/1 tablespoon plain flour	*1 tablespoon all-purpose flour*
1.5 litres/2½ pints stock (beef, chicken, vegetable)	*6¼ cups stock (beef, chicken, vegetable)*
1 × 15 ml spoon/1 tablespoon tomato purée	*1 tablespoon tomato paste*
Dumplings:	Dumplings:
100 g/4 oz self-raising flour	*1 cup self-rising flour*
50 g/2 oz shredded suet	*6 tablespoons shredded suet*
2 × 15 ml spoons/2 tablespoons chopped fresh parsley and thyme	*2 tablespoons chopped fresh parsley and thyme*
salt	*salt*
freshly ground black pepper	*freshly ground black pepper*
4 × 15 ml spoons/4 tablespoons water	*¼ cup water*

Heat the oil in a large saucepan and sauté the bacon, onion, garlic, celery, carrots, mushrooms and green pepper for 10 minutes until lightly browned. Stir in the paprika and flour and cook for 1 minute. Add the stock and tomato purée (paste) and bring to the boil. Cover and simmer for 45 minutes until the vegetables are tender.

To make the dumplings, mix the flour, suet, herbs, salt and pepper to taste in a bowl. Add the water to make a soft dough. Divide into 8 or 12 pieces and shape into balls. Add the dumplings to the soup, cover and simmer for 15 to 20 minutes until they have risen and plumped up. Serve hot, allowing 2 parsley dumplings for each serving.

SERVES 4 TO 6

Goulash Dumpling Soup

Prawn (Shrimp) Pâté

METRIC/IMPERIAL	AMERICAN
275 g/10 oz peeled prawns	*1¼ cups peeled shrimp*
salt	*salt*
freshly ground black pepper	*freshly ground black pepper*
pinch ground mace	*pinch ground mace*
pinch cayenne	*pinch cayenne*
1 × 2.5 ml spoon/½ teaspoon anchovy essence	*½ teaspoon anchovy extract*
50 g/2 oz unsalted butter	*¼ cup unsalted butter*
4 sprigs fresh dill or parsley to garnish	*4 sprigs fresh dill or parsley to garnish*

Blend 225 g/8 oz/1 cup of the prawns (shrimp) with the remaining ingredients until smooth. Transfer to a small saucepan, check seasoning and stir in the remaining prawns (shrimp). Bring just to the boil. Pour into 4 individual cocottes or 1 large china dish. Smooth the top. Chill. Decorate with dill or parsley and serve with hot toast and butter.

SERVES 4

Chicken Liver and Mushroom Pâté

METRIC/IMPERIAL	AMERICAN
100 g/4 oz butter	*½ cup butter*
2 rashers streaky bacon, rinded and chopped	*2 slices streaky bacon, rinded and chopped*
1 onion, peeled and chopped	*1 onion, peeled and chopped*
1 clove garlic, crushed	*1 clove garlic, crushed*
100 g/4 oz mushrooms, sliced	*1 cup sliced mushrooms*
225 g/8 oz chicken livers, cleaned and roughly chopped	*1 cup chicken livers, firmly packed, cleaned and roughly chopped*
sprig fresh thyme or pinch dried thyme	*sprig fresh thyme or pinch dried thyme*
1 bay leaf	*1 bay leaf*
1–2 × 15 ml spoons/1–2 tablespoons brandy	*1–2 tablespoons brandy*
3 × 15 ml spoons/3 tablespoons green peppercorns (optional)	*3 tablespoons green peppercorns (optional)*
salt	*salt*
sprigs fresh thyme (optional garnish)	*sprigs fresh thyme (optional garnish)*

Melt half of the butter in a frying pan and add the bacon, onion, garlic, mushrooms, livers and herbs. Fry for 10 minutes, stirring occasionally until cooked. Spoon into a blender or food processor with the pan juices and the brandy, discarding the bay leaf, and blend until smooth. Stir in 2 × 15 ml spoons/2 tablespoons of the green peppercorns, if using, and add salt to taste. Spoon into a small serving dish (about 450 ml/¾ pint/2 cups) and smooth the top.

Clarify the remaining butter by heating it until it foams, then straining through muslin (cheesecloth). Sprinkle the remaining green peppercorns over the surface of the pâté and pour over the melted clarified butter. Extra small sprigs of fresh thyme may be arranged on top before pouring over the clarified butter, if liked. Chill in the refrigerator until set. Serve with toast or Melba toast.

SERVES 4

Avocado Pâté

METRIC/IMPERIAL	AMERICAN
1 large ripe avocado pear	*1 large ripe avocado pear*
grated rind and juice ½ lemon	*grated rind and juice ½ lemon*
100 g/4 oz full fat soft cheese	*1 cup full fat soft cheese*
1 × 15 ml spoon/1 tablespoon grated onion	*1 tablespoon grated onion*
1 clove garlic, crushed	*1 clove garlic, crushed*
1 teaspoon chopped tarragon	*1 teaspoon chopped tarragon*
few drops Tabasco sauce	*few drops hot pepper sauce*
salt	*salt*
freshly ground black pepper	*freshly ground black pepper*
4 large tomatoes	*4 large tomatoes*
fresh parsley to garnish	*fresh parsley to garnish*
1 × 15 ml spoon/1 tablespoon lumpfish roe (optional)	*1 tablespoon lumpfish roe (optional)*

Cut the avocado pear in half and remove the stone (pit). Scoop out the flesh into a mixing bowl and immediately pour over the lemon rind and juice to prevent the avocado from browning. Mash the avocado roughly with a fork, until fairly smooth. Stir in the cheese, onion, garlic and tarragon. Add the Tabasco sauce (hot pepper sauce), and salt and pepper to taste. Either serve the pâté at once, or place in a dish, cover immediately and chill until required. It will keep for several hours in the refrigerator without browning.

Cut the tops off the tomatoes and scoop out the seeds from the centre. Turn the tomatoes upside down for a minute to drain off the juice. Place the tomatoes on a serving dish or on individual dishes.

Pile the avocado pâté into the centre of the tomatoes. Garnish with parsley, or, for a special occasion, sprinkle the lumpfish roe on to the tops. If preferred, the tomato tops can be replaced. Serve at once.

SERVES 4

Avocado Pâté

Tomatoes Stuffed with Herb-Anchovy Rice

METRIC/IMPERIAL

4 large, ripe tomatoes
salt
225 g/8 oz cooked, long-grain rice
2 × 15 ml spoons/2 tablespoons finely chopped parsley
25 g/1 oz chopped fresh basil or 2 × 15 ml spoons/2 tablespoons dried basil chopped with an extra 2 tablespoons parsley
4 × 15 ml spoons/4 tablespoons olive oil
8 flat, canned anchovy fillets, drained and chopped
4 cloves garlic, crushed
freshly ground black pepper
sugar

AMERICAN

4 large, ripe tomatoes
salt
1½ cups cooked, long-grain rice
2 tablespoons finely chopped parsley
1 cup chopped fresh basil or 2 tablespoons dried basil chopped with an extra ¾ cup parsley
¼ cup olive oil
8 flat, canned anchovy fillets, drained and chopped
4 cloves garlic, crushed
freshly ground black pepper
sugar

Cut a slice from the top of each tomato and set the slices aside. Scoop out the pulp with a sharp-edged spoon, leaving a shell about 1 cm/½ inch thick, and place the pulp in a sieve set over a bowl. Sprinkle inside the shells with salt and stand upside-down on paper towels to drain. Rub the pulp through the sieve. Place rice, parsley, basil, oil, anchovies, garlic and 125 ml/4 oz/½ cup of the tomato pulp in a bowl and mix lightly together. Season to taste with salt and pepper and a dash of sugar.

Stand tomato shells upright in an oiled, shallow baking dish just large enough to hold them (prop them up with crumpled aluminium foil if necessary). Spoon the rice mixture into each shell and cover the tops with the reserved slices. Bake in a preheated moderately hot oven (190°C/375°F, Gas Mark 5) for 10 to 15 minutes, until the tomato shells are slightly softened. Serve hot or cold.

SERVES 4

Salmon Roulade

Salmon Roulade

METRIC/IMPERIAL	AMERICAN
1 × 200 g/7 oz can salmon	*1 can (oz) salmon*
4 eggs, separated	*4 eggs, separated*
1 × 15 ml spoon/1 tablespoon tomato purée	*1 tablespoon tomato paste*
salt	*salt*
freshly ground black pepper	*freshly ground black pepper*
2 × 15 ml spoons/2 tablespoons grated Parmesan cheese	*2 tablespoons grated Parmesan cheese*
Filling:	Filling:
300 ml/½ pint milk	*1¼ cups milk*
1 small onion, peeled and quartered	*1 small onion, peeled and quartered*
2 parsley stalks, finely chopped	*2 parsley stalks, finely chopped*
1 bay leaf	*1 bay leaf*
strip lemon rind	*strip lemon rind*
25 g/1 oz butter	*2 tablespoons butter*
25 g/1 oz plain flour	*¼ cup all-purpose flour*
4 hard-boiled eggs, chopped	*4 hard-cooked eggs*
2 × 15 ml spoons/2 tablespoons chopped fresh dill	*2 tablespoons chopped fresh dill*
2 × 5 ml spoons/2 teaspoons lemon juice	*2 teaspoons lemon juice*
salt	*salt*
pepper	*pepper*
To garnish:	To garnish:
slices cucumber and lemon	*slices cucumber and lemon*
sprigs fresh dill or parsley, or cress	*sprigs fresh dill or parsley, or cress*

Transfer the salmon and juices from the can to a mixing bowl. Remove the black skin and any bones. Mash the salmon to a purée with a fork. Beat in the egg yolks, tomato purée (paste), salt and pepper. Whisk the egg whites until stiff and fold them into the mixture. Line a Swiss roll tin (jelly roll pan) or shallow baking sheet, about 33 × 23 cm/13 × 9 inches, with greaseproof (waxed) paper to come above the sides of the tin and brush with oil. Pour the roulade mixture into the prepared tin and level the surface. Bake near the top of a preheated moderately hot oven (200°C/400°F, Gas Mark 6) for 10 to 15 minutes until the roulade is well risen, firm and golden.

To prepare the filling, pour the milk into a small saucepan and add the onion, parsley, bay leaf and lemon rind. Bring to the boil, remove from the heat and leave to infuse for at least 10 minutes, then strain into a jug. Melt the butter in a saucepan, stir in the flour and then the flavoured milk over a low heat. Bring to the boil, stirring until the sauce thickens and simmer for 2 minutes. Stir in the chopped eggs, dill, lemon juice and salt and pepper to taste.

Just before removing the roulade from the oven, sprinkle a large sheet of greaseproof (waxed) paper with the Parmesan cheese. Turn the roulade on to the paper, remove the tin and peel off the lining paper. Reheat the filling and spread the mixture over the roulade, leaving a 2.5 cm/1 inch margin all the way round. Roll up the roulade like a Swiss roll (jelly roll) by gently lifting the paper so that the roulade falls over into a roll. Lift it on to a serving dish.

Serve immediately or cover and keep warm in the oven for a short time if necessary. Garnish with cucumber and lemon slices and sprigs of parsley or dill, and serve cut into slices.

SERVES 6 TO 8

Variation:
The roulade may also be served cold. To do this invert the roulade on to the greaseproof (waxed) paper and roll up without the filling, but with the greaseproof (waxed) paper inside, and leave to cool. Cover and chill in the refrigerator until required or the next day. For the filling, fold the chopped egg and parsley into 300 ml/½ pint/1¼ cups mixed mayonnaise and soured cream or plain yogurt. Unroll the roulade, remove the paper and spread with the filling and re-roll. To serve, garnish with slices of cucumber and lemon, sprigs of dill and cress and, for a special occasion, rolls of smoked salmon.

Mushrooms and Leeks à la Grecque

METRIC/IMPERIAL	AMERICAN
2 × 15 ml spoons/2 tablespoons oil, preferably olive oil	*2 tablespoons oil, preferably olive oil*
1 large onion, peeled and sliced	*1 large onion, peeled and sliced*
1 large clove garlic, crushed	*1 large clove garlic, crushed*
1 celery stick, sliced	*1 stalk celery, sliced*
225 g/8 oz leeks, sliced	*2 cups leeks, sliced*
150 ml/¼ pint dry white wine	*⅔ cup dry white wine*
225 g/8 oz tomatoes, peeled, quartered and seeds removed	*½ lb tomatoes, peeled, quartered and seeds removed*
salt	*salt*
freshly ground black pepper	*freshly ground black pepper*
1 × 15 ml spoon/1 tablespoon chopped fresh parsley	*1 tablespoon chopped fresh parsley*
1 × 15 ml spoon/1 tablespoon fresh thyme or 1 × 5 ml spoon/1 teaspoon dried thyme	*1 tablespoon fresh thyme or 1 teaspoon dried thyme*
1 bay leaf	*1 bay leaf*
225 g/8 oz button mushrooms	*2 cups button mushrooms*
2 × 15 ml spoons/2 tablespoons chopped fresh parsley to garnish	*2 tablespoons chopped fresh parsley to garnish*

Heat the oil in a large pan and add the onion, garlic, celery and leeks. Sauté gently for 5 minutes without browning. Add the wine, tomatoes, salt and pepper and herbs, and bring to the boil. Add the mushrooms and simmer gently for 10 minutes. Discard bay leaf, leave to cool, then pour into a serving dish and chill. Serve cold, sprinkled with chopped parsley.

SERVES 4

Tuna Fish Mousse

METRIC/IMPERIAL
300 ml/½ pint milk
1 small onion, peeled and quartered
2 parsley stalks
1 bay leaf
strip lemon rind
25 g/1 oz butter
25 g/1 oz plain flour
1 × 200 g/7 oz can tuna fish
150 ml/¼ pint mayonnaise
150 ml/¼ pint plain yogurt
grated rind and juice ½ small lemon
chopped fresh basil
1 × 15 ml spoon/1 tablespoon tomato purée
2 × 5 ml spoons/2 teaspoons anchovy essence
salt
freshly ground black pepper
1 egg, separated
15 g/½ oz powdered gelatine
2 × 15 ml spoons/2 tablespoons water
To garnish:
slices cucumber
100 g/4 oz prawns (optional)

AMERICAN
1¼ cups milk
1 small onion, peeled and quartered
2 parsley stalks
1 bay leaf
strip lemon rind
2 tablespoons butter
¼ cup all-purpose flour
1 can (7 oz) tuna fish
⅔ cup mayonnaise
⅔ cup plain yogurt
grated rind and juice ½ small lemon
chopped fresh basil
1 tablespoon tomato paste
2 teaspoons anchovy extract
salt
freshly ground black pepper
1 egg, separated
2 envelopes unflavored gelatin
2 tablespoons water
To garnish:
slices cucumber
½ cup shrimp (optional)

To make the sauce, pour the milk into a small saucepan, and add the onion, parsley, bay leaf and lemon rind. Bring to the boil, remove from the heat and leave to infuse for at least 10 minutes, then strain. Melt the butter in a saucepan, stir in the flour and then the flavoured milk over a low heat. Bring to the boil, stirring until the sauce is thickened and smooth. Simmer for 2 minutes. Spoon the tuna fish into a mixing bowl, with the juices from the can and mash well with a fork. Beat in the sauce, then the mayonnaise and the yogurt. Stir in the lemon rind and juice, basil, tomato purée (paste), anchovy essence (extract), and salt and pepper to taste. Beat in the egg yolk. Dissolve the gelatine in the water and stir into the mixture. Whisk the egg white until stiff and fold in. Turn into a 900 ml/1½ pint/5 to 6 cup ring or fish mould, or soufflé dish, and chill in the refrigerator until set.

To serve, dip the mould in hot water for a few seconds, then unmould on to a serving plate. Garnish with cucumber, and prawns (shrimp) if using.

SERVES 6 TO 8

Swedish Tomato Cream

METRIC/IMPERIAL
40 g/1½ oz butter
2 onions, peeled and chopped
1 clove garlic, crushed
1 × 397 g/14 oz can tomatoes
250 ml/8 fl oz chicken stock
1 × 15 ml spoon/1 tablespoon fresh dill or 1 × 5 ml spoon/1 teaspoon dried dill
salt
freshly ground black pepper
3 × 15 ml spoons/3 tablespoons mayonnaise
few watercress leaves to garnish

AMERICAN
3 tablespoons butter
2 onions, peeled and chopped
1 clove garlic, crushed
1 can (16 oz) tomatoes
1 cup chicken stock
1 tablespoon fresh dill or 1 teaspoon dried dill
salt
freshly ground black pepper
3 tablespoons mayonnaise
few watercress leaves to garnish

Melt the butter in a saucepan, add the onion and cook gently for 5 minutes. Stir in the garlic, tomatoes with their juice, stock, dill, salt and pepper to taste. Bring to the boil and simmer for 10 minutes. Allow to cool a little, then purée in a blender or food processor until smooth. Mix in the mayonnaise thoroughly. Pour into a bowl, cool, cover and chill. Serve in chilled soup cups, garnished with watercress.

SERVES 4 TO 6

Cucumber Mousse

METRIC/IMPERIAL

15 cm/6 inch piece cucumber
2 × 5 ml spoons/2 teaspoons tarragon or cider vinegar
1 × 2.5 ml spoon/½ teaspoon dried tarragon
275 g/10 oz curd or cream cheese
2.5 × 5 ml spoons/2½ teaspoons gelatine
150 ml/¼ pint good chicken stock
To garnish:
5 × 15 ml spoons/5 tablespoons chicken stock
1 × 2.5 ml spoon/½ teaspoon gelatine
7 cm/3 inch piece cucumber
sprig of tarragon

AMERICAN

6 inch piece cucumber
2 teaspoons tarragon or cider vinegar
½ teaspoon dried tarragon
1¼ cups small curd/cottage cheese or cream cheese
1 envelope, less ½ teaspoon unflavored gelatin
⅔ cup good chicken stock
To garnish:
⅓ cup chicken stock
½ teaspoon unflavoured gelatin
3 inch piece cucumber
sprig of tarragon

Blend the cucumber, vinegar, tarragon and cheese in a blender or food processor until smooth. Dissolve the gelatine in 2 × 15 ml spoons/2 tablespoons of the stock. Cool quickly and add to the cucumber mixture with the remaining stock. Blend and then divide between 6 individual ramekins and chill until set. Once set, prepare the garnish.

Dissolve the gelatine in the stock and cool slightly. Slice the cucumber. Pour a thin layer of gelatine mixture over each dish and garnish with cucumber slices and the tarragon. Chill for a further 30 minutes. Serve with Melba toast.

SERVES 6

Minted Melon and Orange Cocktail

METRIC/IMPERIAL

1 small, ripe honeydew melon or 2 small ogen melons
2 large oranges
5 cm/2 inch piece cucumber, sliced and quartered
2 × 15 ml spoons/2 tablespoons chopped fresh mint
25 g/1 oz toasted almonds or hazelnuts
½ small lettuce, shredded
sprigs fresh mint to garnish

AMERICAN

1 small, ripe honeydew melon, or 2 small ogen melons
2 large oranges
2 inch piece cucumber, sliced and quartered
2 tablespoons chopped fresh mint
1 tablespoon toasted almonds or hazelnuts
½ small head lettuce, shredded
sprigs fresh mint to garnish

Cut the melon into quarters and remove the seeds. Using a round vegetable baller, scoop out the flesh into balls, or cut into small cubes with a knife. Place the melon in a mixing bowl. Cut the peel and pith from the oranges and cut the flesh into segments between the membrane; discard any pips (seeds). Add the orange segments to the melon with any juice left from the oranges. Add the cucumber, mint and nuts, and toss lightly. Chill in the refrigerator until required.

Divide the lettuce between 4 to 6 individual serving dishes or glasses. Spoon in the melon cocktail, pouring over the juice. Serve chilled, garnished with sprigs of fresh mint.

SERVES 4 TO 6

Variation:
If using ogen melons, cut them in half and scoop out the seeds. Scoop out the flesh and mix with the other ingredients and serve the melon cocktail in the melon cases.

Minted Melon and Orange Cocktail;
Swedish Tomato Cream

Pasta & Rice

Tagliatelle alla Bolognese

METRIC/IMPERIAL

2 × 15 ml spoons/2 tablespoons olive oil
2 rashers bacon, rinded and coarsely chopped
1 onion, peeled and chopped
1 tender celery stick, sliced
100 g/4 oz mushrooms, chopped
100 g/4 oz minced beef
50 g/2 oz chicken livers, cleaned and chopped
2 × 15 ml spoons/2 tablespoons tomato purée
120 ml/4 fl oz red wine
250 ml/8 fl oz beef stock
1 × 15 ml spoon/1 tablespoon chopped basil
1 × 15 ml spoon/1 tablespoon oregano
1 × 5 ml spoon/1 teaspoon sugar
pinch nutmeg
salt
freshly ground pepper
225 g/8 oz tagliatelle
knob butter
125 g/4 oz grated Parmesan cheese

AMERICAN

2 tablespoons olive oil
2 slices bacon, rinded and coarsely chopped
1 onion, peeled and chopped
1 tender stalk celery, sliced
1 cup mushrooms, chopped
½ cup ground beef, firmly packed
¼ cup chicken livers, cleaned and chopped
2 tablespoons tomato paste
½ cup red wine
1 cup beef stock or broth
1 tablespoon chopped basil
1 tablespoon oregano
1 teaspoon sugar
pinch nutmeg
salt
freshly ground pepper
½ lb tagliatelle
knob butter
1 cup grated Parmesan cheese

Heat the oil in a large saucepan and gently fry the bacon, onion, celery and mushrooms until soft. Add the meat and chicken livers and continue cooking, stirring frequently, until all the meat is brown. Stir in the tomato purée (paste), then the wine and stock. Add the basil, sugar, nutmeg and salt and pepper to taste. Bring to the boil, stirring, then cover the pan and simmer the sauce for 45 minutes.

Fifteen minutes before the sauce is ready, start to cook the tagliatelle in plenty of boiling salted water. It will take about 10 minutes, and should be tender but still firm to the bite. Drain well, season with salt and pepper to taste and fork through a knob of butter. Arrange in a heated serving dish. Taste the sauce and adjust the seasoning if necessary, then spoon it over the tagliatelle. Serve with a bowl of grated Parmesan cheese handed separately and a tossed green salad.

SERVES 2

Cannelloni

METRIC/IMPERIAL

salt
1 × 15 ml spoon/1 tablespoon vegetable oil
8 sheets wide lasagne
1 quantity Bolognese sauce (see *Tagliatelle alla Bolognese)*
For the cheese sauce:
25 g/1 oz butter
25 g/1 oz flour
300 ml/½ pint hot milk
1 × 1.25 ml spoon/¼ teaspoon ground mace
freshly ground black pepper
50 g/2 oz Cheddar cheese, grated
To finish:
2 × 15 ml spoons/2 tablespoons grated Parmesan cheese
1 × 15 ml spoon/1 tablespoon butter, cut into small pieces

AMERICAN

salt
1 tablespoon vegetable oil
8 pieces wide lasagne noodles
1 quantity Bolognese sauce (see *Tagliatelle alla Bolognese)*
For the cheese sauce:
2 tablespoons butter
¼ cup flour
1¼ cups hot milk
¼ teaspoon ground mace
freshly ground black pepper
½ cup grated Cheddar cheese
To finish:
2 tablespoons grated Parmesan cheese
1 tablespoon butter, cut into small pieces

Bring a large pan of salted water to the boil and stir in the vegetable oil. Cook half the lasagne for 8 to 10 minutes or until *al dente* (tender but firm to the bite). Lift out and pat dry with a clean tea (dish) towel or kitchen paper towels. Repeat this process with the remaining lasagne. Put a spoonful of Bolognese sauce on each sheet (piece) of lasagne and roll up. Place the cannelloni in a baking dish.

To prepare the sauce: melt the butter in a saucepan, stir in the flour and cook for 1 to 2 minutes, stirring constantly. Remove from the heat and gradually add the milk, stirring vigorously. When all the milk is incorporated, return to the heat and bring to the boil, stirring constantly. Lower the heat, add the mace, salt and pepper to taste and the grated cheese. Simmer gently for a few minutes until the sauce is thick, stirring constantly. Coat the cannelloni with the sauce, sprinkle with the Parmesan cheese, dot with butter and put under a preheated hot grill (broiler) for a few minutes or until the top is golden brown. Serve immediately.

SERVES 2

Spaghettini with Tomatoes and Basil

Spaghettini with Tomatoes and Basil

METRIC/IMPERIAL

450 g/1 lb spaghettini or vermicelli
Sauce:
4 large ripe tomatoes
2 cloves garlic, crushed
3 × 15 ml spoons/3 tablespoons chopped fresh parsley
15 g/$\frac{1}{2}$ oz chopped fresh basil
4 × 15 ml spoons/4 tablespoons olive oil
salt
freshly ground pepper

AMERICAN

1 lb spaghettini or vermicelli
Sauce:
4 large ripe tomatoes
2 cloves garlic, crushed
3 tablespoons chopped fresh parsley
$\frac{1}{4}$ cup chopped fresh basil
$\frac{1}{4}$ cup olive oil
salt
freshly ground pepper

Peel, seed, and coarsely chop the tomatoes. Place with the garlic, parsley, basil and oil in a blender or food processor and blend to a purée. Heat gently in a saucepan to boiling point, then taste and season well. Meanwhile, cook the pasta in plenty of boiling salted water for about 8 to 10 minutes, until tender but still firm to the bite (*al dente*). Drain well and toss at once with the fresh tomato sauce. Serve with crusty French bread.

SERVES 4 TO 6

Note: When fresh basil is not in season, substitute 1 × 15 ml spoon/1 tablespoon chopped fresh oregano or marjoram.

Pesto with Noodles

METRIC/IMPERIAL

50 g/2 oz fresh basil
2 cloves garlic
25 g/1 oz pine nuts
salt
25 g/1 oz freshly grated Parmesan cheese
2 × 15 ml spoons/2 tablespoons olive oil
450 g/1 lb white tagliatelle or other noodles

AMERICAN

$\frac{3}{4}$ cup fresh basil
2 cloves garlic
$\frac{1}{4}$ cup pine nuts
salt
$\frac{1}{4}$ cup freshly grated Parmesan cheese
2 tablespoons olive oil
1 lb white tagliatelle or other noodles

Put the basil into a mortar and pound for 2 minutes. Add the garlic, pine nuts and salt to taste and pound until smooth. Stir in the Parmesan cheese and pound until the mixture is quite smooth. When the pesto is quite thick, gradually add the olive oil, drop by drop, so that the finished sauce is the consistency of creamed butter. Cook the pasta in boiling salted water for 9 minutes. Drain and return to the pan. Stir in the pesto sauce and heat through. Pile the mixture into a warmed serving dish and serve at once.

SERVES 4

Lasagne Verde

METRIC/IMPERIAL
225 g/8 oz green lasagne
25 g/1 oz grated Parmesan cheese
Meat sauce:
1 × 15 ml spoon/1 tablespoon oil
1 onion, peeled and chopped
1 clove garlic, crushed
1 celery stick, chopped
50 g/2 oz streaky bacon, rinded and chopped
350 g/12 oz minced beef
25 g/1 oz plain flour
300 ml/½ pint beef stock
2 × 15 ml spoons/2 tablespoons tomato purée
2 × 5 ml spoons/2 teaspoons chopped fresh oregano or 1 × 5 ml spoon/1 teaspoon dried oregano
salt
freshly ground black pepper
Béchamel sauce:
450 ml/¾ pint milk
1 onion, peeled and quartered
2 sprigs parsley
1 bay leaf
25 g/1 oz butter
25 g/1 oz plain flour
1 × 1.25 ml spoon/¼ teaspoon grated nutmeg
salt
freshly ground black pepper

AMERICAN
½ lb green lasagne noodles
¼ cup grated Parmesan cheese
Meat sauce:
1 tablespoon oil
1 onion, peeled and chopped
1 clove garlic, crushed
1 stalk celery, chopped
3 slices streaky bacon, rinded and chopped
1½ cups ground beef, firmly packed
¼ cup all-purpose flour
1¼ cups beef stock
2 tablespoons tomato paste
2 teaspoons chopped fresh oregano, or 1 teaspoon dried oregano
salt
freshly ground black pepper
Béchamel sauce:
2 cups milk
1 onion, peeled and quartered
2 sprigs parsley
1 bay leaf
2 tablespoons butter
¼ cup all-purpose flour
¼ teaspoon grated nutmeg
salt
freshly ground black pepper

To make the meat sauce, heat the oil in a large saucepan and fry the onion, garlic, celery and bacon for 5 minutes. Add the meat and continue frying for 5 minutes, stirring until the meat is browned. Stir in the flour, then add the stock, tomato purée (paste), oregano, and salt and pepper to taste. Bring to the boil, stirring, then cover and simmer gently for 30 minutes, stirring occasionally.

Meanwhile, make the Béchamel sauce: pour the milk into a saucepan and add the onion, parsley and bay leaf. Bring the milk to the boil, remove the saucepan from the heat and leave to infuse for at least 10 minutes. Melt the butter in a saucepan and stir in the flour. Strain the flavoured milk through a sieve into the saucepan. Bring to the boil, stirring until the sauce is smooth and thick. Simmer for 2 minutes, then add the nutmeg and salt and pepper to taste.

Lower the sheets (pieces) of pasta one at a time into a large pan of boiling salted water for 5 to 15 minutes (depending on whether the pasta is fresh or dried) until just tender. Adding a little oil to the pan helps to prevent the lasagne from sticking together. Cook the lasagne in batches if necessary. Drain the lasagne and spread the sheets (pieces) to dry on a clean tea (dish) towel. Arrange layers of meat, pasta and Béchamel sauce in an ovenproof dish, finishing with a layer of Béchamel sauce. Sprinkle the top with Parmesan cheese. (The lasagne may be prepared in advance, chilled and baked when required.)

Bake in a preheated moderate oven (190°C/375°F, Gas Mark 5) for 30 minutes until bubbling and golden brown on top. Serve at once.

SERVES 4

Above: Lasagne Verde; Opposite: Pasta Shell Salad

Linguine with Courgette (Zucchini)-Anchovy Sauce

METRIC/IMPERIAL	AMERICAN
450 g/1 lb linguine (see Note)	*1 lb linguine (see Note)*
150 g/5 oz butter	*½ cup plus 2 tablespoons butter*
3 × 15 ml spoons/3 tablespoons olive oil	*3 tablespoons olive oil*
6 firm young courgettes, thinly sliced	*6 firm young zucchini, thinly sliced*
6 flat anchovy fillets, finely chopped	*6 flat anchovy fillets, finely chopped*
3 large, ripe tomatoes, peeled, seeded and chopped	*3 large, ripe tomatoes, peeled, seeded and chopped*
salt	*salt*
freshly ground pepper	*freshly ground pepper*
2 × 5 ml spoons/2 tablespoons finely chopped fresh parsley	*2 tablespoons finely chopped fresh parsley*
50 g/2 oz freshly grated Parmesan cheese	*½ cup freshly grated Parmesan cheese*

Cook the linguine in plenty of boiling, salted water until tender but still firm.

Meanwhile, heat 75 g/3 oz/⅓ cup butter and the oil in a large, heavy frying pan (skillet) and add the courgettes (zucchini). Stir over medium heat until barely tender, about 3 minutes. Add the anchovies and tomatoes and cook a further few minutes until tomatoes are softened. Taste and season with salt and pepper – be careful with the salt, as the anchovies are salty.

Drain the linguine and place in a heated serving bowl. Add the remaining butter, cut into small pieces, the parsley and grated cheese and toss to combine. Pour the sauce over and toss lightly again. Serve at once on heated plates.

SERVES 6

Note: Linguine are narrow, flat ribbons of pasta. If unavailable, use tagliatelle or other flat noodles.

Pasta Shell Salad

METRIC/IMPERIAL	AMERICAN
225 g/8 oz pasta shells	*½ lb pasta shells*
salt	*salt*
150 ml/¼ pint French dressing with 1 × 2.5 ml spoon/½ teaspoon marjoram added	*⅔ cup French dressing with ½ teaspoon marjoram added*
1 × 15 ml spoon/1 tablespoon anchovy essence	*1 tablespoon anchovy extract*
1 × 5 ml spoon/1 teaspoon tomato purée	*1 teaspoon tomato paste*
225 g/8 oz white fish, cooked and flaked (cod, haddock, coley or whiting)	*1 cup white fish, cooked and flaked (cod, haddock, coley or whiting)*
1 × 200 g/7 oz can tuna fish, drained and flaked	*1 can (7 oz) tuna fish, drained and flaked*
100 g/4 oz peeled prawns	*⅔ cup peeled shrimp*
freshly ground black pepper	*freshly ground black pepper*
1 lettuce, washed and drained	*1 head lettuce, washed and drained*
To garnish:	To garnish:
unpeeled prawns	*unpeeled shrimp*
slices lemon	*slices lemon*
1 × 15 ml spoon/1 tablespoon chopped fresh parsley and marjoram	*1 tablespoon chopped fresh parsley and marjoram*

Cook the pasta in a large pan of boiling salted water for 10 to 15 minutes until just tender. Place the drained pasta in a bowl. Mix the French dressing with the anchovy essence (extract) and tomato purée (paste) and pour half of this over the pasta. Toss well and leave until cold. Add the white fish, tuna fish and prawns (shrimp) to the pasta. Pour over the remaining dressing and toss lightly. Season to taste with pepper. Leave to marinate for at least 30 minutes in a cold place.

Line a serving dish, or individual dishes, with lettuce leaves and pile the pasta and fish salad in the centre. Garnish with unpeeled prawns (shrimp), lemon slices and herbs.

SERVES 4

Curried Rice

METRIC/IMPERIAL

100 g/4 oz ghee or clarified butter
3 onions, peeled and finely sliced
2 × 5 ml spoons/2 teaspoons turmeric
4 × 5 ml spoons/4 teaspoons curry powder
1 kg/2 lb long-grain rice
1.6 litres/2$\frac{3}{4}$ pints chicken stock
12 peppercorns
4 whole cloves
8 cardamom pods, bruised
1 stick cinnamon
4 × 5 ml spoons/4 teaspoons salt
225 g/8 oz cooked peas (optional)

AMERICAN

$\frac{1}{2}$ cup ghee or clarified butter
3 onions, peeled and finely sliced
2 teaspoons turmeric
4 teaspoons curry powder
2 lb long-grain rice
7 cups chicken stock
12 peppercorns
4 whole cloves
8 cardamom pods, bruised
1 stick cinnamon
4 teaspoons salt
1$\frac{1}{2}$ cups cooked peas (optional)

Heat the ghee or clarified butter in a large heavy saucepan or flameproof casserole. Sauté half the onions until golden brown, add the turmeric and curry powder and stir well for a minute. Add the rice and fry for a few minutes, stirring, until golden in colour. Add boiling stock, peppercorns, spices, salt and remaining onions. Stir well, cover and cook over a gentle heat for about 20 minutes. Turn off the heat and keep covered until ready to serve. A few minutes before serving, uncover pan to allow steam to escape. Fluff up with a fork and garnish with peas, if liked.

SERVES 12

Scampi Risotto

METRIC/IMPERIAL

450 g/1 lb prawns
1.2 litres/2 pints water
1 fish head or small, whole fish
1 celery stick, sliced
1 small onion, peeled and sliced
1 small carrot, peeled and sliced
1 bay leaf
salt
freshly ground pepper
65 g/2$\frac{1}{2}$ oz butter
2 × 15 ml spoons/2 tablespoons olive oil
1 clove garlic, crushed
175 g/6 oz raw, round-grain rice
good pinch each ground cinnamon, nutmeg and cloves
1 × 15 ml spoon/1 tablespoon finely chopped fresh parsley
3 × 15 ml spoons/3 tablespoons freshly grated Parmesan cheese

AMERICAN

1 lb shrimp
5 cups water
1 fish head or small, whole fish
1 stalk celery, sliced
1 small onion, peeled and sliced
1 small carrot, peeled and sliced
1 bay leaf
salt
freshly ground pepper
5 tablespoons butter
2 dablespoons olive oil
1 clove garlic, crushed
1 cup raw, short-grain rice
good pinch each ground cinnamon, nutmeg and cloves
1 tablespoon finely chopped fresh parsley
3 tablespoons freshly grated Parmesan cheese

If the prawns are still in their shells, peel, devein and place the shells and heads in a large saucepan with the water, fish heads or whole fish, celery, onion, carrot, bay leaf, and salt and pepper to taste. Bring to the boil, simmer for 30 minutes, then strain into a measuring jug.

Heat 50 g/2 oz butter and the oil in a wide, heavy saucepan or deep frying pan (skillet). Sauté the garlic over medium heat for 1 to 2 minutes, then add the rice and stir until golden. Add 220 ml/8 fl oz/1 cup reserved fish stock, cover the pan and simmer for 10 minutes, or until liquid is absorbed. Add another 600 ml/1 pint/2$\frac{1}{2}$ cups of the fish stock and simmer, covered, for a further 10 minutes. Add the raw prawns (shrimp) and continue cooking, covered, for 5 to 6 minutes longer or until the prawns (shrimp) are pink and the stock has been absorbed. Gently stir in the spices, remaining butter, parsley and cheese. Taste for seasoning and serve at once on heated plates.

SERVES 4

Creamy Noodles with Fresh Herbs

METRIC/IMPERIAL

450 g/1 lb tagliatelle
2 cloves garlic, crushed
50 g/2 oz butter
120 ml/4 fl oz single cream
2 × 15 ml spoons/2 tablespoons chopped fresh parsley
2 × 15 ml spoons/2 tablespoons snipped chives
1 × 15 ml spoon/1 tablespoon chopped fresh basil
1 × 15 ml spoon/1 tablespoon chopped fresh oregano or marjoram
salt
freshly ground pepper
To serve:
freshly grated Parmesan or Cheddar cheese

AMERICAN

1 lb tagliatelle
2 cloves garlic, crushed
$\frac{1}{4}$ cup butter
$\frac{1}{2}$ cup light cream
2 tablespoons chopped fresh parsley
2 tablespoons chopped chives
1 tablespoon chopped fresh basil
1 tablespoon chopped fresh oregano or marjoram
salt
freshly ground pepper
To serve:
freshly grated Parmesan or Romano cheese

Cook the pasta in plenty of boiling salted water until tender but still firm to the bite (*al dente*), for about 10 minutes. Drain thoroughly and toss with the crushed garlic and butter. Heat the cream just to boiling point, and add the chopped herbs. Season to taste with salt and plenty of freshly ground pepper. Pour over the buttered pasta and toss gently but thoroughly until mixed. Serve at once in heated bowls, and pass freshly grated cheese at the table.

SERVES 4

Scampi Risotto; Creamy Noodles with Fresh Herbs

Eggs

Italian Eggs

METRIC/IMPERIAL	AMERICAN
25 g/1 oz parsley sprigs	*¼ cup parsley sprigs*
1 × 5 ml spoon/1 teaspoon fresh marjoram or pinch dried marjoram	*1 teaspoon fresh marjoram or pinch dried marjoram*
1 clove garlic, crushed	*1 clove garlic, crushed*
6 black olives, stoned	*6 pitted ripe olives*
1 shallot, peeled	*1 shallot, peeled*
2 anchovy fillets	*2 anchovy fillets*
freshly ground black pepper	*freshly ground black pepper*
120 ml/4 fl oz olive oil	*½ cup olive oil*
salt	*salt*
6 hard-boiled eggs, shelled and sliced	*6 hard-cooked eggs, shelled and sliced*
tomato wedges to garnish	*tomato wedges to garnish*
chopped parsley to garnish	*chopped parsley to garnish*

Blend the parsley, marjoram, garlic, olives, shallot, anchovy fillets and pepper in a blender or food processor until smooth, then add the oil. Adjust the seasoning. Arrange the eggs on a serving dish and pour the sauce over them. Garnish with tomato wedges and sprinkle with parsley.

SERVES 4

Spicy Egg Curry

METRIC/IMPERIAL	AMERICAN
8 hard-boiled eggs	*8 hard-cooked eggs*
2 cloves garlic, crushed	*2 cloves garlic, crushed*
1 large onion, peeled and finely chopped	*1 large onion, peeled and finely chopped*
1 × 15 ml spoon/1 tablespoon oil	*1 tablespoon oil*
1 × 5 ml spoon/1 teaspoon each ground coriander and ground cumin	*1 teaspoon each ground coriander and ground cumin*
1 × 2.5 ml spoon/½ teaspoon chilli powder (or to taste)	*½ teaspoon chili powder (or to taste)*
2 × 15 ml spoons/2 tablespoons sesame seeds	*2 tablespoons sesame seeds*
1 × 2.5 ml spoon/½ teaspoon salt	*½ teaspoon salt*
250 ml/8 fl oz plain yogurt	*1 cup plain yogurt*
2 × 15 ml spoons/2 tablespoons lemon juice	*2 tablespoons lemon juice*

Shell the eggs. Cook the garlic and onion in oil until soft. Add the remaining ingredients, except the yogurt and lemon juice, and cook for 1 minute, stirring. Blend in the yogurt and juice and cook for 5 minutes. Cut the eggs in half lengthwise, add to the sauce, and heat through. Serve with boiled rice.

SERVES 4

Spiced Scrambled Eggs

METRIC/IMPERIAL
8 eggs
4 tomatoes, peeled and chopped
1 × 5 ml spoon/1 teaspoon salt
50 g/2 oz ghee or clarified butter
1 medium onion, peeled and sliced
2 green chillis, seeded and chopped
1 × 5 ml spoon/1 teaspoon turmeric
1 × 5 ml spoon/1 teaspoon ground coriander

AMERICAN
8 eggs
4 tomatoes, peeled and chopped
1 teaspoon salt
¼ cup ghee or clarified butter
1 medium onion, peeled and sliced
2 green chillis, seeded and chopped
1 teaspoon turmeric
1 teaspoon ground coriander

Put the eggs, tomatoes and salt in a bowl and beat well. Melt the ghee or clarified butter in a pan, add the onion and fry gently until soft. Add the chillis and spices and fry for 2 minutes, stirring constantly. Add the beaten egg mixture and stir with a wooden spoon until the eggs are scrambled. Serve hot on toast for breakfast, or as a light supper.
SERVES 4

Spicy Egg Curry; Spiced Scrambled Eggs

Courgette (Zucchini) Flan

METRIC/IMPERIAL	AMERICAN
175 g/6 oz shortcrust pastry	*6 oz basic pie dough*
450 g/1 lb courgettes, topped and tailed	*1 lb zucchini, cleaned*
2 eggs	*2 eggs*
300 ml/½ pint milk	*1¼ cups milk*
salt	*salt*
freshly ground black pepper	*freshly ground black pepper*
grated nutmeg	*grated nutmeg*
1 clove garlic, crushed	*1 clove garlic, crushed*
1 × 5 ml spoon/1 teaspoon tomato purée	*1 teaspoon tomato paste*
dash Tabasco sauce	*dash hot pepper sauce*

Roll out the pastry (pie dough) and use to line an 18 cm/7 inch flan tin (pie pan). Line the pastry (pie dough) with greaseproof (waxed) paper and weigh down with dried beans. Bake blind in a moderately hot oven (200°C/400°F, Gas Mark 6) for 15 minutes. Remove foil and beans and bake for a further 5 to 10 minutes. Remove and set aside to cool.

Slice the courgettes (zucchini) and blanch in boiling salted water for 1 minute, drain well and set aside. Blend the eggs, milk, salt, pepper, nutmeg, garlic, tomato purée (paste) and Tabasco (hot pepper) sauce. Arrange courgette (zucchini) slices in the pastry case (pie shell). Pour in the egg mixture. Bake in a moderately hot oven (200°C/400°F, Gas Mark 6) for 30 to 40 minutes or until set and golden.

SERVES 4

Venetian Flan

METRIC/IMPERIAL	AMERICAN
100 g/4 oz shortcrust pastry	*¼ lb basic pie dough*
50 g/2 oz Gruyère cheese	*2 oz Gruyère cheese*
75 g/3 oz Cheddar cheese	*3 oz Cheddar cheese*
1 onion, peeled	*1 onion, peeled*
1 × 15 ml spoon/1 tablespoon olive oil	*1 tablespoon olive oil*
225 g/8 oz Italian salami, cut into cubes	*½ lb Italian salami, cut into cubes*
100 g/4 oz ham, cut into strips	*¼ lb ham, cut into strips*
3 eggs	*3 eggs*
300 ml/½ pint top of the milk	*1¼ cups half and half*
salt	*salt*
freshly ground black pepper	*freshly ground black pepper*
grated nutmeg	*grated nutmeg*

Roll out the pastry (pie dough) on a floured board and use to line a 20 cm/8 inch flan tin (pie pan). Grate the Gruyère and set aside. Grate the Cheddar and set aside. (Keep the cheeses separate.) Slice the onion. Heat the oil in a frying pan (skillet) and add the onion. Cook gently until soft. Stir in the salami and cook for 5 minutes. Put the onion and salami into the pastry case (pie shell) and sprinkle with half the Gruyère and half the Cheddar. Arrange the ham strips over the top of the cheeses.

In a bowl, beat together the eggs, milk (half and half) and remaining cheese, and add salt, pepper and nutmeg to taste. Pour over the cheese and ham. Bake in a moderately hot oven (200°C/400°F, Gas Mark 6) and bake for a further 20 minutes or until the custard is set and lightly golden.

SERVES 6

Quiche Lorraine

METRIC/IMPERIAL	AMERICAN
175 g/6 oz shortcrust pastry	*6 oz basic pie dough*
4 rashers streaky bacon	*4 slices streaky bacon*
75 g/3 oz Swiss or Gruyère cheese, sliced	*3 oz Swiss or Gruyère cheese, sliced*
4 rashers streaky bacon	*2 eggs*
75 g/3 oz Swiss or Gruyère cheese, sliced	*1 teaspoon flour*
2 eggs	*pinch grated nutmeg*
1 × 5 ml spoon/1 teaspoon flour	*½ teaspoon salt*
pinch grated nutmeg	*pinch cayenne*
1 × 2.5 ml spoon/½ teaspoon salt	*½ cup cream*
pinch cayenne	*½ cup milk*
120 ml/4 fl oz cream	*2 tablespoons butter, melted*
120 ml/4 fl oz milk	*watercress or bacon rolls to garnish*
25 g/1 oz butter, melted	
watercress or bacon rolls to garnish	

Roll out the pastry (dough) on a lightly floured board and use to line a 20 cm/8 inch flan tin (pie pan).

Remove the rind from the bacon and grill (broil) until crisp. Cut into 1 cm/½ inch squares, and cut the cheese the same size. Place in layers in the pastry case (pie shell). Beat the eggs with the flour, nutmeg, salt, cayenne, cream and milk until just combined (over-beating causes bubbles on top). Stir in the melted butter. Strain over the bacon and cheese and bake in a preheated moderately hot oven (200°C/400°F, Gas Mark 6) for 18 minutes. Reduce the heat to moderate (180°C/350°F, Gas Mark 4) and bake for a further 20 minutes, or until a knife inserted in the centre comes out clean. Serve the quiche warm, garnished with watercress or grilled (broiled) bacon rolled up and secured with cocktail sticks (toothpicks).

SERVES 4 TO 6

Courgette Flan; Quiche Lorraine

Eggs en Cocotte with Mushrooms

METRIC/IMPERIAL
salt
freshly ground black pepper
pinch paprika
25 g/1 oz butter
50 g/2 oz mushrooms, chopped
4 eggs
150 ml/$\frac{1}{4}$ pint single cream
chopped fresh parsley to garnish

AMERICAN
salt
freshly ground black pepper
pinch paprika
2 tablespoons butter
$\frac{1}{2}$ cup chopped mushrooms
4 eggs
$\frac{2}{3}$ cup light cream
chopped fresh parsley to garnish

The eggs will continue cooking after the dish has been removed from the oven, so be careful not to overcook them. Lightly butter 4 cocotte or ramekin dishes, or a shallow ovenproof dish, and sprinkle with salt, pepper and paprika. Melt the butter in a saucepan and sauté the mushrooms until softened. Divide the mushrooms between the dishes or put into the large dish. Break an egg into each dish if using individual ones, and place the dishes or dish in a roasting tin half-filled with water. Bake in the centre of a preheated moderate oven (180°C/350°F, Gas Mark 4) for about 10 minutes until the whites are barely set, and the yolks still soft. Meanwhile, heat the cream in a saucepan, but do not let it boil. Remove the dishes or dish from the oven and spoon the cream over each egg. Garnish with chopped parsley. Serve with hot toast.
SERVES 4

Variation:
Use 100 g/4 oz/$\frac{1}{2}$ cup chopped cooked ham or chicken instead of mushrooms, or simply bake the eggs without a filling.

Eggs Benedict

METRIC/IMPERIAL	AMERICAN
40 g/1½ oz butter	3 tablespoons butter
40 g/1½ oz plain flour	5 tablespoons all-purpose flour
300 ml/½ pint milk and 150 ml/¼ pint double cream, or 450 ml/¾ pint milk	1¼ cups milk and ⅔ cup heavy cream, or 2 cups milk
salt	salt
freshly ground black pepper	freshly ground black pepper
450 g/1 lb flaked, cooked cod	1 lb flaked, cooked cod
1 clove garlic, crushed	1 clove garlic, crushed
1 × 15 ml spoon/1 tablespoon chopped fresh parsley	1 tablespoon chopped fresh parsley
2 × 15 ml spoons/2 tablespoons cooking oil	2 tablespoons cooking oil
2 slices white bread, crusts removed and cut into triangles for croûtes	2 slices white bread, crusts removed and cut into triangles for croûtes
4 eggs	4 eggs
finely chopped fresh parsley to garnish	finely chopped fresh parsley to garnish

Melt the butter in a pan, stir in the flour and cook for 2 minutes. Gradually stir in the milk and cream, if using, over a low heat. Bring to the boil, stirring continuously. Add salt and pepper to taste. Put 5 × 15 ml spoons/5 tablespoons/⅓ cup of the sauce in a bowl with the flaked fish and stir in the crushed garlic and parsley. Heat the oil and fry the triangles of bread. Drain them well on kitchen paper towels.

Poach the eggs until just set and dry them on kitchen paper towels. Gently reheat the fish mixture and the remaining sauce in 2 separate saucepans. Spoon the fish mixture over the base of a serving dish. Top with the poached eggs and pour over the remaining sauce. Garnish with the croûtes and chopped parsley. Serve immediately.

SERVES 4

Eggs Milton

METRIC/IMPERIAL	AMERICAN
50 g/2 oz butter	¼ cup butter
225 g/8 oz tomatoes, peeled and sliced	½ lb tomatoes, peeled and sliced
2 slices white bread, crusts removed, and cut into triangles for croûtes	2 slices white bread, crusts removed, and cut into triangles for croûtes
2 spring onions, trimmed and chopped	2 scallions, trimmed and chopped
100 g/4 oz button mushrooms, sliced	¼ lb button mushrooms, sliced
½ green pepper, cored, seeded and diced	½ green pepper, seeded and diced
4 eggs	4 eggs
4 × 15 ml spoons/4 tablespoons milk	¼ cup milk
salt	salt
freshly ground black pepper	freshly ground black pepper
1 × 5 ml spoon/1 teaspoon dried thyme	1 teaspoon dried thyme

Heat one third of the butter in a frying pan (skillet) and sauté the tomato slices for a few minutes. Place in the base of an ovenproof serving dish and keep warm. Wipe out the pan (skillet) and melt a further third of the butter in it. Fry the bread triangles on both sides and drain well. Put them aside. Gently sauté the spring onions (scallions), mushrooms and green pepper until soft. Take off the heat. In a basin, beat together the eggs and milk. Add salt and pepper to taste, and the thyme. Melt the remaining butter in a saucepan and cook the eggs gently, stirring from time to time, until they become creamy and thickened. Stir the cooked vegetables into the eggs and spoon this mixture over the tomatoes. Arrange the croûtes down each side of the dish and serve immediately.

SERVES 4

Eggs Florentine

METRIC/IMPERIAL
225 g/8 oz packet frozen spinach
knob butter
pinch ground mace
Sauce:
25 g/1 oz butter
25 g/1 oz plain flour
300 ml/½ pint milk
pinch dry English mustard
50 g/2 oz grated Cheddar cheese
salt
freshly ground black pepper
4 eggs
grated nutmeg to garnish

AMERICAN
½ lb package frozen spinach
knob butter
pinch ground mace
Sauce:
2 tablespoons butter
¼ cup all-purpose flour
1¼ cups milk
pinch dry English mustard
½ cup grated Cheddar cheese
salt
freshly ground black pepper
4 eggs
grated nutmeg to garnish

Cook the spinach with a knob of butter and a pinch of mace until completely thawed and heated through. Drain the spinach and spoon it over the base of a serving dish. To make the sauce, melt the butter in a pan, stir in the flour and cook for 2 minutes. Gradually stir in the milk over a low heat. Bring to the boil, stirring, then add the mustard, half the cheese and salt and pepper to taste. Remove from the heat.

Poach the eggs until just set and dry them on kitchen paper. Arrange the poached eggs over the spinach. Reheat the sauce and pour over the eggs. Sprinkle the remaining cheese and nutmeg over the top and place in a preheated moderate oven (180°C/350°F, Gas Mark 4) for 10 to 15 minutes.

SERVES 4

Opposite: Eggs Benedict; Below: Eggs Florentine

Fish

Shellfish in Rich Herb Sauce

METRIC/IMPERIAL

1 lobster, weighing about 450 g/1 lb, lightly boiled
3 × 15 ml spoons/3 tablespoons olive oil
1 onion, peeled and finely chopped
1 red pepper, cored, seeded, and thinly sliced
1 green pepper, cored, seeded and thinly sliced
2 cloves garlic, chopped
2 × 5 ml spoons/2 teaspoons paprika
2 baby squid, cleaned and cut into rings (optional)
4 tomatoes, peeled and chopped
12 blanched almonds, crushed
3 pinches powdered saffron
1 bay leaf
200 ml/$\frac{1}{3}$ pint dry white wine
3 × 15 ml spoons/3 tablespoons brandy
juice of 1 lemon
200 ml/$\frac{1}{3}$ pint water
salt
freshly ground black pepper
12 prawns, unpeeled
8 mussels, scrubbed and bearded
8 clams or cockles, scrubbed
chopped parsley to garnish

AMERICAN

1 lobster, weighing about 1 lb, lightly boiled
3 tablespoons olive oil
1 onion, peeled and finely chopped
1 red pepper, seeded and thinly sliced
1 green pepper, seeded and thinly sliced
2 cloves garlic, chopped
2 teaspoons paprika
2 baby squid, cleaned and cut into rings (optional)
4 tomatoes, peeled and chopped
12 blanched almonds, crushed
3 pinches powdered saffron
1 bay leaf
$\frac{7}{8}$ cup dry white wine
3 tablespoons brandy
juice of 1 lemon
$\frac{7}{8}$ cup water
salt
freshly ground black pepper
12 shrimp, unshelled
8 mussels, scrubbed and bearded
8 clams or cockles, scrubbed
chopped parsley to garnish

Slit the lobster in half lengthwise. Discard the head and stomach sac and the dark intestinal vein which runs along the inside of the body. Twist off the large claws and crack them. Put on one side with the rest of the fish.

Heat the oil in a large flameproof casserole. Add the onion, peppers, garlic, paprika and squid, if used. Cook gently for 10 to 15 minutes. Add the tomatoes, almonds, saffron and bay leaf, then stir in the wine, brandy, lemon juice and water. Stir well and allow to bubble for 1 to 2 minutes over a high heat. Season to taste with salt and pepper. Add all the shellfish to the pan, cover and cook over a low heat for about 15 minutes. Discard any mussels or clams or cockles that have not opened. Correct the seasoning and sprinkle with parsley before serving.

SERVES 4

Prawn (Shrimp) Curry

METRIC/IMPERIAL

450 g/1 lb prawns, peeled and deveined
juice 1 lime or $\frac{1}{2}$ lemon
1 × 1.25 ml spoon/$\frac{1}{4}$ teaspoon saffron, soaked in 1 × 15 ml spoon/1 tablespoon hot water
5 cloves garlic, crushed
3 curry leaves or 1 small bay leaf
2 × 5 ml spoons/2 teaspoons grated root ginger
2 cloves
1 × 5 ml spoon/1 teaspoon ground cinnamon
1 × 2.5 ml spoon/$\frac{1}{2}$ teaspoon fenugreek
1 × 2.5 ml spoon/$\frac{1}{2}$ teaspoon ground cardamom
1 × 1.25 ml spoon/$\frac{1}{4}$ teaspoon cayenne or to taste
2 × 15 ml spoons/2 tablespoons peanut oil
2 large, ripe tomatoes, peeled, seeded and chopped
*220 ml/8 fl oz coconut milk (*see *page 92)*
salt

AMERICAN

1 lb shrimp, shelled and deveined
juice 1 lime or $\frac{1}{2}$ lemon
$\frac{1}{4}$ teaspoon saffron, soaked in 1 tablespoon hot water
5 cloves garlic, crushed
3 curry leaves or 1 small bay leaf
2 teaspoons grated ginger root
2 cloves
1 teaspoon ground cinnamon
$\frac{1}{2}$ teaspoon fenugreek
$\frac{1}{2}$ teaspoon ground cardamom
$\frac{1}{4}$ teaspoon cayenne or to taste
2 tablespoons peanut oil
2 large tomatoes, peeled, seeded and chopped
*1 cup coconut milk (*see *page 92)*
salt

Mix the prawns (shrimp) with the lime or lemon juice and the saffron and water in a large bowl. Add the garlic, curry leaves or bay leaf, ginger and spices; then cover and stand at room temperature for 1 hour. Heat the peanut oil in a wok or heavy frying pan (skillet), add prawn (shrimp) mixture and sauté briskly for 2 minutes or until prawns turn pink. Remove prawn (shrimp) mixture with a slotted spoon and set aside. Add the tomatoes to the pan and sauté gently for 3 minutes, then add coconut milk and simmer until mixture thickens a little. Stir in salt to taste. Return prawn (shrimp) mixture to pan, heat through and serve at once.

SERVES 2 TO 3 WITH RICE

Note: If saffron is unobtainable or too expensive, substitute 1 × 5 ml spoon/1 teaspoon turmeric.

Marinated Seafood with Oranges

Marinated Seafood with Oranges

METRIC/IMPERIAL
450 g/1 lb white fish fillets
225 g/8 oz scallops, dark beards removed
4 × 15 ml spoons/4 tablespoons vegetable oil
1 small green pepper, cored and seeded
2 large oranges, thinly peeled (reserve rind)
2 spring onions, trimmed and finely chopped
4 × 15 ml spoons/4 tablespoons vinaigrette
chopped fresh parsley
Marinade:
5 × 15 ml spoons/5 tablespoons olive oil
4 × 15 ml spoons/4 tablespoons orange juice
1 × 15 ml spoon/1 tablespoon lime or lemon juice
1 × 15 ml spoon/1 tablespoon red wine vinegar
1.5 × 5 ml spoons/1½ teaspoons salt
freshly ground black pepper
2 cloves garlic, crushed
1 × 5 ml spoon/1 teaspoon grated root ginger
pinch cayenne

AMERICAN
1 lb white fish fillets
½ lb scallops, bearded
¼ cup vegetable oil
1 small green pepper, seeded
2 large oranges, thinly peeled (reserve rind)
2 scallions, trimmed and finely chopped
¼ cup vinaigrette
chopped fresh parsley
Marinade:
⅓ cup olive oil
¼ cup orange juice
1 tablespoon lime or lemon juice
1 tablespoon red wine vinegar
1½ teaspoons salt
freshly ground black pepper
2 cloves garlic, crushed
1 teaspoon grated root ginger
pinch cayenne

Skin the fish fillets, cut them into strips about 10 × 3 cm/4 × 1¼ inches and remove any bones. Dry fish and scallops with kitchen paper towels. Heat the vegetable oil in frying pan (skillet) until it gives off a slight haze and lightly brown the fish strips, about 2 minutes each side. Using a slotted fish slice, remove fish to a shallow serving dish. Add scallops to the pan (skillet) and cook on one side for 10 seconds, turn over and cook the other side for 10 seconds. Remove and add to the fish. Cut the pepper and reserved orange rind into thin strips and sprinkle over the seafood with the chopped spring onions (scallions). Mix together all the marinade ingredients and pour over. Cover the dish with cling film (plastic wrap) and refrigerate overnight.

Next day, remove all white pith from the oranges and cut them into thick slices, removing any pips (seeds). Drizzle vinaigrette over the slices and chill, covered, for 1 hour. Arrange orange slices round the marinated seafood, then sprinkle the seafood with chopped parsley. Serve chilled, with plenty of crusty bread to mop up the delicious juice.

SERVES 4

Fish Yucatan-Style

METRIC/IMPERIAL

4 large fish fillets
4 cloves garlic, crushed
1 × 5 ml spoon/1 teaspoon dried oregano
1 × 2.5 ml spoon/½ teaspoon ground cumin
salt
freshly ground pepper
4 × 15 ml spoons/4 tablespoons orange juice
120 ml/4 fl oz olive oil
2 tomatoes, peeled and chopped
1 onion, peeled and thinly sliced
½ small hot chilli, seeded and chopped
chopped fresh parsley or coriander

AMERICAN

4 large fish fillets
4 cloves garlic, crushed
1 teaspoon dried oregano
½ teaspoon ground cumin
salt
freshly ground pepper
¼ cup orange juice
½ cup olive oil
2 tomatoes, peeled and chopped
1 onion, peeled and thinly sliced
½ small hot chili, seeded and chopped
chopped fresh parsley or coriander

Wipe over the fish fillets, skin and cut into serving-sized pieces. Arrange on a large plate or glass dish. Combine the garlic, oregano, cumin, salt and pepper to taste, and orange juice and pour over the fish pieces. Allow to marinate for 30 minutes.

Choose a flameproof baking dish just big enough to hold the fillets comfortably. Coat the bottom of the dish with half the oil. Arrange the fillets in the dish and pour over the marinade. Combine the tomatoes with the sliced onion and chopped chilli and spoon over the fish. Sprinkle with the remaining olive oil. Cover the dish with aluminium foil and simmer over a gentle heat for 20 minutes. Sprinkle the fish with chopped parsley or coriander and serve.

SERVES 4 TO 6

Cider-Soused Mackerel

METRIC/IMPERIAL

4 small mackerel
salt and black pepper
1 onion, peeled and thinly sliced
1 × 15 ml spoon/1 tablespoon lemon juice
1 eating apple, peeled, cored and sliced
6 peppercorns
1 × 5 ml spoon/1 teaspoon fennel seeds
2 bay leaves
300 ml/½ pint dry cider

AMERICAN

4 small mackerel
salt and black pepper
1 onion, peeled and thinly sliced
1 tablespoon lemon juice
1 eating apple, peeled, cored and sliced
6 peppercorns
1 teaspoon fennel seeds
2 bay leaves
1¼ cups hard cider

Remove the heads, fins and guts from the mackerel. Clean the fish and remove the backbones without removing the tails. Season the flesh with salt and pepper, then roll up each fish towards the tail. Place the rolled mackerel in a shallow ovenproof dish, with the tails pointing upwards. Scatter the onion slices over and around the fish. Add the lemon juice to the apple and put the slices in the dish, with the peppercorns, fennel and bay leaves. Pour over the cider and cover the dish. Bake in a preheated moderate oven (180°C/350°F, Gas Mark 4) for 30 to 40 minutes until the fish is tender. Serve cold.

SERVES 2

Baked Fish with Herbs and Mussel Sauce

METRIC/IMPERIAL

1.5–1.75 kg/3–4 lb fish
lemon juice
salt
50 g/2 oz butter, melted
100 g/4 oz soft white breadcrumbs
1 sprig marjoram, chopped, or pinch dried marjoram
2 × 15 ml spoons/2 tablespoons chopped fresh parsley
freshly ground black pepper
cayenne to taste
2 rashers bacon, cut in two
Mussel sauce:
25 g/1 oz butter
4 × 5 ml spoons/4 teaspoons flour
120 ml/4 fl oz fish stock
120 ml/4 fl oz single cream
12 cooked mussels or 1 small can
salt
white pepper

AMERICAN

3–4 lb fish
lemon juice
salt
¼ cup butter, melted
2 cups soft white bread crumbs
1 sprig marjoram, chopped, or pinch dried marjoram
2 tablespoons chopped fresh parsley
freshly ground black pepper
cayenne to taste
2 slices bacon, cut in two
Mussel sauce:
2 tablespoons butter
4 teaspoons flour
½ cup fish stock
½ cup light cream
12 cooked mussels or 1 small can
salt
white pepper

Clean the fish, leaving the head and tail intact. Rub with lemon juice and sprinkle the body cavity with salt. Heat the butter in a frying pan (skillet) and lightly brown the crumbs. Add the herbs, salt, pepper and cayenne and mix together. Stuff the fish loosely with the mixture and close the cavity with skewers and string. Line a baking dish with aluminium foil by using a double thickness and allowing it to overlap at both ends. This will make handles, so it is easy to lift out the cooked fish without breaking it. Grease the aluminium foil, place the fish on it and arrange the bacon on top. Bake, uncovered, in a moderately hot oven (200°C/400°F, Gas Mark 6) for 30 to 40 minutes or until the fish flakes easily when tested with a fork.

While the fish is cooking, make the sauce. Melt the butter in a small saucepan. Blend in the flour with a whisk and add the fish stock. Lightly whisk over a gentle heat until thickened. Add the cream gradually until a shiny, smooth sauce results. Add the mussels and heat through (do not allow to boil). Taste and adjust the seasoning.

Using the foil as handles, transfer the fish to a heated platter. Pour over the mussel sauce and serve.

SERVES 4 TO 6

Grilled Oriental Fish

Grilled Oriental Fish

METRIC/IMPERIAL
6 thick serving-size pieces of white fish fillets
2 × 15 ml spoons/2 tablespoons soy sauce
2 slices root ginger, peeled and chopped
1 × 1.25 ml spoon/¼ teaspoon 5-spice powder
2 × 15 ml spoons/2 tablespoons oil
pinch sugar
pinch pepper
2 × 15 ml spoons/2 tablespoons dry white wine
coriander (Chinese parsley) sprigs and spring onion brushes to garnish

AMERICAN
6 thick serving-size pieces of white fish fillets
2 tablespoons soy sauce
2 slices ginger root, peeled and chopped
¼ teaspoon 5-spice powder
2 tablespoons oil
pinch sugar
pinch pepper
2 tablespoons dry white wine
coriander (Chinese parsley) sprigs and scallion brushes to garnish

Wipe over the fish and remove any visible scales or bones. Combine the remaining ingredients, except for the garnish, in a flat dish. Place the fish in the dish and turn about to coat. Leave for 1 hour, turning the fish once.

Line the grill (broiler) pan with aluminium foil, heat under the grill (broiler), then put in the fish, skin side up. Pour over half the marinade and grill (broil) at high heat for 4 to 5 minutes. Pour over the remaining marinade and grill (broil) for a further 4 to 5 minutes. Transfer to a heated platter and pour over any marinade remaining in the pan. Garnish with coriander (Chinese parsley) sprigs and spring onion (scallion) brushes (cut the leaves lengthwise almost to the base and stand in ice-cold water until they curl) and serve immediately.
SERVES 6

Variation:
Grilled curried fish Omit the soy sauce and substitute 1 × 2.5 ml spoon/½ teaspoon curry powder for the 5-spice powder. Continue as above.

Grilled Fish au Fromage

METRIC/IMPERIAL

4 × 150–175 g/5–6 oz steaks or portions of white fish, skinned if necessary
salt
freshly ground black pepper
25 g/1 oz butter
1 × 5 ml spoon/1 teaspoon dried rosemary
100 g/4 oz finely grated Cheddar cheese, or a mixture of Gruyère and Parmesan
1 × 15 ml spoon/1 tablespoon (scant) French mustard
2–3 × 15 ml spoons/2–3 tablespoons single cream
2 firm tomatoes, sliced
watercress sprigs to garnish

AMERICAN

4 × 5–6 oz steaks or portions of white fish, skinned if necessary
salt
freshly ground black pepper
2 tablespoons butter
1 teaspoon dried rosemary
1 cup grated Cheddar cheese, or a mixture of Gruyere and Parmesan
1 tablespoon (scant) Dijon-style mustard
2–3 tablespoons light cream
2 firm tomatoes, sliced
watercress sprigs to garnish

Wipe the fish with damp kitchen paper towels and season generously with salt and pepper. Preheat the grill (broiler) and melt the butter with half the rosemary in a shallow flameproof dish, large enough to hold the fish in a single layer. Turn the fish in the melted butter, then grill (broil) under a moderate heat for about 4 to 5 minutes (under a low heat for 7 to 8 minutes if the fish is still frozen). Meanwhile, put the cheese, mustard and remaining rosemary into a basin and beat in enough cream to make a soft mixture. Turn the fish carefully, spread them evenly with the cheese mixture and continue grilling (broiling), very gently, for 5 to 6 minutes. When the surface is golden, but not overbrowned, arrange 2 slices of tomato on each portion and grill for a further minute. Serve from the dish, garnished at the last moment with sprigs of watercress.

SERVES 4

Fish Pie

METRIC/IMPERIAL

450 g/1 lb potatoes, peeled, boiled and drained, then mashed with 25 g/1 oz butter, salt and pepper and enough milk to make a creamy spreading consistency

Filling:

450 g/1¼ lb thick white fish fillets
300 ml/½ pint milk
1 thick slice onion
good pinch each dried rosemary and thyme
1 small bay leaf
4 peppercorns
salt
40 g/1½ oz butter
25 g/1 oz plain flour
50 g/2 oz grated cheese
225 g/8 oz tomatoes, peeled and chopped, or 50 g/2 oz peeled prawns
2 hard-boiled eggs, sliced
2 × 15 ml spoons/2 tablespoons chopped fresh parsley (optional)
freshly ground pepper

AMERICAN

1 lb potatoes, peeled, boiled and drained, then mashed with 2 tablespoons butter, salt and pepper and enough milk to make a creamy spreading consistency

Filling:

1¼ lb thick white fish fillets
1¼ cups milk
1 thick slice onion
good pinch each dried rosemary and thyme
1 small bay leaf
4 peppercorns
salt
3 tablespoons butter
¼ cup all-purpose flour
½ cup grated cheese
½ lb tomatoes, peeled and chopped, or ⅓ cup peeled shrimp
2 hard-cooked eggs, sliced
2 tablespoons chopped fresh parsley (optional)
freshly ground pepper

Rinse the fish under cold water, cut each fillet into 2 or 3 pieces and put into a saucepan. Add the milk, onion, herbs, peppercorns and a little salt. Bring slowly to simmering point, then cover and cook very gently for 12 to 15 minutes. Strain off the liquid and reserve for the cheese sauce. Melt 25 g/1 oz/2 tablespoons butter in a clean saucepan, stir in the flour and cook gently for 1 to 2 minutes. Gradually stir in the reserved cooking liquid. When smoothly blended, stir until boiling, then simmer gently for several minutes.

Meanwhile, remove any skin or bones from the pieces of fish and flake the flesh roughly. Discard the onion, bay leaf and peppercorns. Stir into the sauce half the cheese, all the tomatoes or prawns (shrimp), hard-boiled (hard-cooked) eggs, parsley if used, flaked fish and salt and pepper to taste. Mix gently over a low heat until thoroughly heated through. Pour the mixture into a flameproof pie dish, spread the prepared potato topping over the top to cover it completely, and mark the surface with a fork. Sprinkle with the remaining cheese, dot with flakes of the remaining butter and grill gently for a few minutes until the surface is golden and crisp.

SERVES 4

Variation:

Aberdeen fish pie Use smoked cod or haddock fillet instead of the white fish and omit the prawns (shrimp) and cheese.

Provençal Poached Fish

METRIC/IMPERIAL

4 whole fish, each weighing about 250 g/8 oz or 4 large fillets (e.g. red mullet, bream, snapper or whiting)
2 kg/4 lb mussels, beards removed and scrubbed
fresh basil to garnish

Sauce:

300 ml/½ pint olive oil
1 clove garlic, crushed
1 tomato, peeled, seeded and chopped
1 × 5 ml spoon/1 teaspoon finely chopped fresh fennel
1 × 2.5 ml spoon/½ teaspoon finely chopped fresh rosemary
1 × 15 ml spoon/1 tablespoon finely chopped fresh basil
pinch paprika
pinch ground coriander (Chinese parsley)
salt
freshly ground black pepper

Court bouillon:

350 ml/12 fl oz dry white wine
1 × 15 ml spoon/1 tablespoon wine vinegar
450 ml/¾ pint water
pinch salt
freshly ground pepper
bouquet garni
sprig each rosemary, basil and fennel
2 slices orange
2 slices lemon

AMERICAN

4 whole fish, each weighing about ½ lb or 4 large fillets (e.g. red mullet, bream, snapper, whiting)
4 lb mussels, beards removed and scrubbed
fresh basil to garnish

Sauce:

1⅓ cups olive oil
1 clove garlic, crushed
1 tomato, peeled, seeded and chopped
1 teaspoon finely chopped fresh fennel
½ teaspoon finely chopped fresh rosemary
1 tablespoon finely chopped fresh basil
pinch paprika
pinch ground coriander (Chinese parsley)
salt
freshly ground black pepper

Court bouillon:

1½ cups dry white wine
1 tablespoon wine vinegar
2 cups water
pinch salt
freshly ground pepper
bouquet garni
sprig each rosemary, basil and fennel
2 slices orange
2 slices lemon

Make the sauce 2 or 3 days in advance. Mix all the ingredients together, seasoning to taste with salt and pepper. Cover and leave in a cool place (not the refrigerator) until needed.

Put all the ingredients for the court bouillon into a shallow pan big enough to hold the fish in one layer. Bring to the boil, partially cover and simmer very gently for 1 hour. Add the fish and mussels, cover and poach (the water should not bubble) for 5 minutes or until the mussels open (discard any that do not open). Remove the mussels and keep warm; continue cooking the fish, if necessary, just until the flesh turns white and flakes at the touch of a fork.

Lift the fish out carefully with a slotted fish slice and arrange on a large, heated oval platter. Arrange the mussels in their shells round the platter, garnish with fresh basil and pour the sauce over the fish. Serve immediately.

SERVES 4

Fish Pie; Grilled Fish au Fromage

Fish Fillets Provençale

METRIC/IMPERIAL

750 g/1½ lb white fish fillets, e.g. haddock, whiting, cod or coley, skinned
2 × 15 ml spoons/2 tablespoons flour seasoned with salt, pepper and dried mixed herbs
5 × 15 ml spoons/5 tablespoons olive oil
1 large onion, peeled, halved and thinly sliced
1–2 cloves garlic, crushed
450 g/1 lb tomatoes, peeled, seeded and chopped, or 1 × 397 g/14 oz can tomatoes, drained and chopped
2 × 15 ml spoons/2 tablespoons black or green olives (optional)
1 × 5 ml spoon/1 teaspoon caster sugar
salt
freshly ground black pepper
1 × 15 ml spoon/1 tablespoon chopped fresh chives or chervil

AMERICAN

1½ lb white fish fillets, e.g. haddock, whiting, cod or coley, skinned
2 tablespoons flour seasoned with salt, pepper and dried mixed herbs
⅓ cup olive oil
1 large onion, peeled, halved and thinly sliced
1–2 cloves garlic, crushed
1 lb tomatoes, peeled, seeded and chopped, or 1 can (16 oz) tomatoes, drained and chopped
2 tablespoons black or green olives (optional)
1 teaspoon sugar
salt
freshly ground black pepper
1 tablespoon chopped fresh chives or chervil

Cut the fish into roughly 2.5 cm/1 inch cubes. Coat the fish in the seasoned flour, shaking off any surplus flour. Heat 2 × 15 ml spoons/2 tablespoons of the oil in a frying pan (skillet) and sauté the onion very gently for 6 to 8 minutes, until soft and golden. Add the garlic and sauté for another minute, then add the tomatoes, olives, if using, sugar, and salt and pepper to taste. Stir for several minutes until the tomatoes begin to soften (if using fresh), then cover the pan and remove from the heat.

Meanwhile, heat the remaining oil in a large frying pan (skillet) and, when sizzling hot, put in the pieces of fish and fry them over a moderate heat for about 10 minutes, turning frequently, until cooked through and lightly browned. Using a slotted fish slice, transfer the fish to a hot, shallow serving dish. Spoon the vegetables over the fish and sprinkle with chives or chervil.

SERVES 4 TO 6

Sesame Fish Steaks

METRIC/IMPERIAL

3 large fish steaks or fillets
salt
25 g/1 oz butter
100 g/4 oz soft breadcrumbs
pinch freshly ground pepper
4 × 15 ml spoons/4 tablespoons toasted sesame seeds
1 × 2.5 ml spoon/½ teaspoon fresh thyme, crumbled
1 × 5 ml spoon/1 teaspoon salt

AMERICAN

3 large fish steaks or fillets
salt
2 tablespoons butter
2 cups soft bread crumbs
pinch freshly ground pepper
4 tablespoons toasted sesame seeds
½ teaspoon fresh thyme, crumbled
1 teaspoon salt

Dry the fish steaks with kitchen paper towels and place in a buttered baking dish. Sprinkle the steaks with a pinch of salt and dot each with 2 × 5 ml spoons/2 teaspoons of the butter. Combine the remaining ingredients and sprinkle the breadcrumb mixture thickly over the steaks. Bake, uncovered, in a moderate oven (180°C/350°F, Gas Mark 4) for 15 to 20 minutes or until the fish flakes easily when tested with a fork. Serve with hot bread and a green salad.

SERVES 6

Salmon Trout in Aspic

METRIC/IMPERIAL

1 × 1.5 kg/3 lb salmon trout
salt
freshly ground black pepper
oil
600 ml/1 pint aspic jelly
To garnish:
spray fresh tarragon, fennel or dill
3 medium tomatoes, halved, scooped out and filled with cooked peas (optional)
3 hard-boiled eggs, halved, yolks sieved and creamed with mayonnaise, then piled back into whites
½ cucumber, thinly sliced
½ pint mayonnaise
2 × 15 ml spoons/2 tablespoons chopped fresh herbs such as tarragon and dill

AMERICAN

3 lb salmon trout
salt
freshly ground black pepper
oil
2½ cups aspic jelly
To garnish:
spray fresh tarragon, fennel or dill
3 medium tomatoes, halved, scooped out and filled with cooked peas (optional)
3 hard-cooked eggs, halved, yolks sieved and creamed with mayonnaise, then piled back into whites
½ cucumber, thinly sliced
½ pint mayonnaise
2 tablespoons chopped fresh herbs such as tarragon and dill

Wipe the fish with damp kitchen paper towels, scrape the body cavity clean and sprinkle it with salt and pepper. Lay the fish on a large piece of well-oiled aluminium foil and twist the foil edges together to form a loose but watertight parcel. Place the parcel on a baking sheet and bake in the centre of a preheated moderate oven (180°C/350°F, Gas Mark 4) for 45 minutes. Meanwhile, make up the aspic jelly and leave to cool.

When the fish is cooked, remove the parcel from the oven and leave, unopened, to allow it to cool a little. While the fish is still warm, open the parcel and skin the fish. To do this, cut the skin around the head and across the tail and peel it away from the flesh. Roll the fish over and repeat on the other side. Carefully transfer the fish to a flat serving dish. When the aspic is on the point of setting (if necessary, stir it over crushed ice until it coats the back of a metal spoon), spoon a thin film of jelly over the fish and leave to set. Garnish the fish with a spray of herbs, coat with a second layer of aspic and leave to set again. Chill the remaining aspic until stiff. Chop the stiff aspic into small pieces and arrange the pieces along either side of the fish. Set the filled tomatoes, if using, and eggs alternately in the aspic and border the dish with overlapping slices of cucumber. Stir the chopped herbs into the mayonnaise and serve separately.

SERVES 6

Smoked Haddock Kedgeree

METRIC/IMPERIAL

350 g/12 oz smoked haddock fillets
75 g/3 oz butter
1 medium onion, peeled and finely sliced
1 × 5 ml spoon/1 teaspoon curry powder
100 g/4 oz long-grain rice
25 g/1 oz currants (optional)
300 ml/½ pint water
freshly ground black pepper
1–2 × 5 ml spoons/1–2 teaspoons lemon juice
salt, if necessary
1 × 15 ml spoon/1 tablespoon chopped fresh summer savory or parsley
2 hard-boiled eggs, quartered lengthwise

AMERICAN

¾ lb smoked haddock fillets
¼ cup plus 2 tablespoons butter
1 medium onion, peeled and finely sliced
1 teaspoon curry powder
8 tablespoons long-grain rice
3 tablespoons currants (optional)
1¼ cups water
freshly ground black pepper
1–2 teaspoons lemon juice
salt, if necessary
1 tablespoon chopped fresh summer savory or parsley
2 hard-cooked eggs, quartered lengthwise

Put the haddock fillets in a dish, cover them with boiling water and leave for 5 minutes. Drain, skin and divide the fillets into small pieces. Heat 25 g/1 oz/2 tablespoons of the butter in a saucepan and sauté the onion gently for 5 minutes, until soft but not browned. Stir in the curry powder and cook for a minute, then stir in the rice, currants, if using, and the water. Bring to the boil, reduce the heat, cover tightly and simmer very gently for 15 minutes. Add the haddock and continue cooking gently, stirring frequently with a fork to prevent the mixture sticking to the pan, until all the liquid has been absorbed. Stir in the remaining butter and season to taste with pepper, lemon juice and, if necessary, salt. Pile the kedgeree into a hot serving dish, sprinkle with summer savory or parsley and arrange the hard-boiled (hard-cooked) eggs around the edge.

SERVES 3 TO 4

Salmon Trout in Aspic

Fried Mackerel with Tamarind Sauce

METRIC/IMPERIAL	AMERICAN
4 medium mackerel	*4 medium mackerel*
2 × 15 ml spoons/2 tablespoons vegetable oil	*2 tablespoons vegetable oil*
15 g/½ oz tamarind pulp	*½ oz tamarind pulp*
3 cloves garlic, peeled and finely chopped	*3 cloves garlic, peeled and finely chopped*
2 × 15 ml spoons/2 tablespoons grated fresh ginger	*2 tablespoons grated fresh ginger*
3 × 15 ml spoons/3 tablespoons water	*3 tablespoons water*
1 × 5 ml spoon/1 teaspoon sugar	*1 teaspoon sugar*
To serve:	To serve:
few spring onions, chopped	*few scallions, chopped*
1 cucumber, skinned and cut into 1 cm/½ inch slices	*1 cucumber, skinned and cut into ½ inch slices*

Clean the fish, but do not remove the skin. Wrap the fish together in well-buttered aluminium foil, then bake in a preheated cool oven (150°C/300°F, Gas Mark 2) for 45 minutes until tender. Unwrap the fish, then leave until cool and dry.

Heat the oil in a wok or deep frying pan (skillet), add the fish and fry gently until golden brown. Remove from the pan (skillet) carefully and drain, reserving the pan (skillet) for the sauce. Transfer the fish to a warmed serving dish and keep hot. To make the sauce, first make some tamarind water: soak the tamarind pulp in 150 ml/¼ pint/⅔ cup water for 5 to 10 minutes. Squeeze, strain and reserve the water.

Add the garlic to the pan (skillet) in which the fish was fried and fry over high heat until light brown. Add the ginger and fry for 1 minute. Stir in the water, sugar and 3 tablespoons of tamarind water. Heat through, then pour over the fish. Sprinkle with the spring onions (scallions). Serve hot, with the cucumber as a side dish.

SERVES 4

Mackerel with Caper Dressing

METRIC/IMPERIAL	AMERICAN
6 × 15 ml spoons/6 tablespoons oil	*6 tablespoons oil*
1 large clove garlic, crushed	*1 large clove garlic, crushed*
juice 1 large lemon	*juice 1 large lemon*
75 g/3 oz capers, rinsed and lightly crushed	*½ cup capers, rinsed and lightly crushed*
salt	*salt*
freshly ground black pepper	*freshly ground black pepper*
4 fresh mackerel, cleaned and heads removed	*4 fresh mackerel, cleaned and heads removed*
2 × 15 ml spoons/2 tablespoons chopped fresh chives or parsley	*2 tablespoons chopped fresh chives or parsley*

Mix together the oil, garlic, lemon juice, capers, salt and pepper to taste in a bowl, cover and leave to allow the flavours to blend. Before cooking, slash the fish 3 times diagonally on each side, sprinkle with a little salt and pepper and arrange side by side on the grill (broiler) rack. Spoon the dressing over the fish. Cook under a preheated, moderately hot grill (broiler) for about 5 minutes each side, turning once and basting with the dressing from time to time. If necessary, increase the heat towards the end to brown and crisp the skin. Lift out the fish with a slotted fish slice on to a serving plate. Add the chives or parsley to the pan juices and spoon over the mackerel.

SERVES 4

Trout with Hazelnuts

METRIC/IMPERIAL	AMERICAN
4 × 175 g/6 oz trout, cleaned, heads and tails left on, fins removed	*4 × 6 oz trout, cleaned, heads and tails left on, fins removed*
salt	*salt*
freshly ground black pepper	*freshly ground black pepper*
flour for coating	*flour for coating*
good pinch ground nutmeg	*good pinch ground nutmeg*
1 × 15 ml spoon/1 tablespoon oil	*1 tablespoon oil*
50 g/2 oz unsalted butter	*¼ cup unsalted butter*
75 g/3 oz hazelnuts	*½ cup hazelnuts*
25 g/1 oz salted butter	*2 tablespoons salted butter*
4 × 15 ml spoons/4 tablespoons dry white breadcrumbs	*4 tablespoons dry white breadcrumbs*
2 × 15 ml spoons/2 tablespoons snipped chives or chopped fresh parsley	*2 tablespoons chopped chives or fresh parsley*
1 lemon, quartered, to garnish	*1 lemon, quartered, to garnish*

Wash the trout, pat them dry with kitchen paper towels and season them inside and out with salt and pepper. (If using frozen trout, allow time to thaw). Just before cooking, roll the trout in the flour and nutmeg, coating them evenly. Heat the oil and unsalted butter in a large, heavy frying pan (skillet) and, when the butter ceases to foam, put in the trout and cook gently for 12 to 15 minutes, turning carefully halfway through cooking. Meanwhile, spread the hazelnuts in the grill (broiler) pan and toast them gently for a few minutes until the skins burst, then rub them in a rough cloth to remove the skins. Chop the nuts coarsely.

When the fish are cooked through and golden, lift them out carefully, arrange side by side on a hot serving dish and keep hot. Add the remaining butter to the fat remaining in the frying pan (skillet) – if it has overbrowned, wipe out the pan and start again, using 50 g/2 oz/¼ cup salted butter. When the butter is hot, add the nuts and enough breadcrumbs to absorb all the fat. Fry fairly briskly, stirring, until golden brown and crisp. Stir in the chives or parsley with a little salt and pepper, and scatter immediately over the trout. Garnish with lemon wedges and serve at once with boiled potatoes tossed in butter.

SERVES 4

Mackerel with Caper Dressing; Trout with Hazelnuts

Soused Fish

METRIC/IMPERIAL
6 small mullet or herring
1 onion, peeled and sliced
2 bay leaves
1 clove
4 allspice berries or peppercorns
1 × 5 ml spoon/1 teaspoon salt
120 ml/4 fl oz vinegar
water to cover

AMERICAN
6 small mullet or herring
1 onion, peeled and sliced
2 bay leaves
1 clove
4 allspice berries or peppercorns
1 teaspoon salt
$\frac{1}{2}$ cup vinegar
water to cover

Clean, scale and remove the fish heads. Cut off the fillets and remove any bones. Place slices of onion on the centre of each fillet and roll up, skin side out, from head to tail and fix with a cocktail stick (toothpick). Place the rolled fish in a heavy flameproof casserole or pot with the bay leaves, clove, allspice or peppercorns and salt. Pour over the vinegar and just cover with water. Cover and cook over a low heat for 1–1$\frac{1}{2}$ hours or until the fish flakes easily when tested with a fork.

Transfer the fish to a deep serving dish so that the fish can be covered with liquid. Strain over sufficient cooking liquid to cover the fish. Cool, then chill in the refrigerator, where the liquor will set into a soft jelly. Serve with salad burnet or a cucumber salad.

SERVES 2

Meat

Catalan Beef Stew

METRIC/IMPERIAL

1 kg/2 lb topside of beef
oil or lard for frying
4 rashers back bacon, chopped
1 medium onion, peeled and sliced
2 carrots, peeled and sliced
50 g/2 oz mushrooms, sliced
1 clove garlic, crushed
pinch each dried parsley, dried thyme, dried rosemary and grated nutmeg
1 bay leaf
1 × 210 g/7$\frac{1}{2}$ oz can tomatoes
1 × 5 ml spoon/1 teaspoon black treacle
300 ml/$\frac{1}{2}$ pint cider
salt
pepper

AMERICAN

2 lb round of beef
oil or lard for frying
4 slices back bacon, chopped
1 medium onion, peeled and sliced
2 carrots, peeled and sliced
$\frac{1}{2}$ cup mushrooms, sliced
1 clove garlic, crushed
pinch each dried parsley, dried thyme, dried rosemary and grated nutmeg
1 bay leaf
1 can (7 oz) tomatoes
1 teaspoon molasses
1$\frac{1}{4}$ cups hard cider
salt
pepper

Brown the meat on all sides in the oil or lard in a frying pan (skillet), then drain on kitchen paper towels. Lightly fry the bacon, onion and carrots in the same pan (skillet), drain and transfer to an ovenproof pot or casserole. Add the mushrooms, garlic, herbs and nutmeg, and place the meat on top. Mix together the tomatoes, treacle, cider and salt and pepper to taste and pour over the joint. Cook in a hot oven (220°C/425°F, Gas Mark 7) for 10 minutes and then turn the oven down to moderate (160°C/325°F, Gas Mark 3) and cook for a further 1$\frac{1}{2}$ to 2 hours or until the meat is tender. Lift the meat on to a warmed serving dish; leave whole or cut into thick slices. Quickly sieve the sauce or blend in a blender or food processor. Reheat in a separate pan, adjusting consistency and seasoning if necessary.

SERVES 4 TO 6

Fried Steak with Chilli

METRIC/IMPERIAL

450 g/1$\frac{1}{4}$ lb rump steak or topside of beef
2 × 5 ml spoons/2 teaspoons ground coriander
2 × 15 ml spoons/2 tablespoons tamarind water (see Fried Mackerel *with Tamarind Sauce, Fish chapter)*
1 × 5 ml spoon/1 teaspoon brown sugar
salt
freshly ground black pepper
8 red chillis, seeded and chopped
4 shallots, peeled and chopped
2 cloves garlic, peeled and chopped
6 × 15 ml spoons/6 tablespoons vegetable oil
1 × 5 ml spoon/1 teaspoon lemon juice

AMERICAN

1$\frac{1}{4}$ lb top round steak or top round of beef
2 teaspoons ground coriander
2 tablespoons tamarind water (see Fried Mackerel *with Tamarind Sauce, Fish chapter)*
1 teaspoon brown sugar
salt
freshly ground black pepper
8 red chilies, seeded and chopped
4 shallots, peeled and chopped
2 cloves garlic, peeled and chopped
6 tablespoons vegetable oil
1 teaspoon lemon juice

Slice the meat thinly across the grain, then cut the slices into 5 cm/2 inch squares. Arrange in a single layer on a plate and sprinkle with the coriander, tamarind water, sugar, and salt and pepper to taste. Press each piece with your hands so that the spices are thoroughly absorbed into the meat, then spread the slices out on the plate again. Leave to stand for 2 to 3 hours.

Put the chillis, shallots and garlic in a mortar and pound until broken, but not reduced to a paste. Heat the oil in a heavy frying pan (skillet). Add the meat and fry until evenly browned and cooked through. Remove from the pan with a slotted spoon and keep hot. Add the pounded mixture to the oil remaining in the pan and sauté for 2 to 3 minutes, stirring constantly. Return the meat to the pan and stir to coat with the spice mixture. Add the lemon juice and salt to taste and stir well. Serve hot, with rice and a tomato and cucumber salad, garnished with borage.

SERVES 4

Provencal Beef Stew

Provencal Beef Stew

METRIC/IMPERIAL

- *3 × 15 ml spoons/3 tablespoons olive oil*
- *2 medium onions, peeled and sliced*
- *175 g/6 oz piece unsmoked streaky bacon, cut into 1 cm/$\frac{1}{2}$ inch cubes*
- *1.5 kg/3 lb piece boneless braising beef: top rump, topside or de-fatted and rolled brisket*
- *1 × 15 ml spoon/1 tablespoon plain flour*
- *salt*
- *freshly ground black pepper*
- *4 large tomatoes, peeled and quartered*
- *2 carrots, peeled and sliced*
- *2 cloves garlic, crushed*
- *2 thinly pared strips orange rind, 1 bay leaf, 1 sprig thyme, 2 sprigs parsley, tied together for bouquet garni*
- *150 ml/$\frac{1}{4}$ pint robust red wine*
- *50 g/2 oz small black olives, rinsed (optional)*

AMERICAN

- *3 tablespoons olive oil*
- *2 medium onions, peeled and sliced*
- *6 oz piece unsmoked streaky bacon, cut into $\frac{1}{2}$ inch cubes*
- *3 lb piece boneless braising beef: top round steak, round rump roast or de-fatted and rolled brisket*
- *1 tablespoon all-purpose flour*
- *salt*
- *freshly ground black pepper*
- *4 large tomatoes, peeled and quartered*
- *2 carrots, peeled and sliced*
- *2 cloves garlic, crushed*
- *2 thinly pared strips orange rind, 1 bay leaf, 1 sprig thyme, 2 sprigs parsley, tied together for bouquet garni*
- *$\frac{2}{3}$ cup robust red wine*
- *$\frac{1}{2}$ cup small ripe olives, rinsed (optional)*

Heat the oil in a flameproof casserole into which the meat fits fairly closely. Add the onions and sauté gently for 5 minutes, then add the cubed bacon and cook gently until the fat begins to run. Meanwhile, wipe the meat with damp kitchen paper towels and dust lightly with flour, well seasoned with salt and pepper. Increase the heat a little, put the meat into the pan and cook until lightly browned on each side. Add the tomatoes, carrots, garlic, bouquet garni, a little salt and several grinds of pepper. Pour in the wine. Bring to the boil, allow to simmer for a few minutes, then cover the pan tightly and transfer to a preheated cool oven (150°C/300°F, Gas Mark 2) and cook for about 4 hours or until the meat is tender when pierced with a skewer.

Turn the meat half way through cooking and add the olives, if using, 30 minutes before the end. To serve, remove the trussing strings and arrange the meat on a hot serving dish, and either leave whole or slice as much as required. Skim off any fat from the gravy, remove the solid ingredients with a slotted spoon and arrange them around the meat. Remove and discard the bouquet garni. Concentrate the rest of the gravy by boiling briskly for a few minutes, then taste and adjust the seasoning and pour it over the meat. Serve with creamed potatoes and a green vegetable or follow with a green salad.

SERVES 8

Mexican Beef Kebabs

METRIC/IMPERIAL

4 × 15 ml spoons/4 tablespoons oil
1 small onion, peeled and chopped
4 × 15 ml spoons/4 tablespoons red wine vinegar
1 × 2.5 ml spoon/½ teaspoon each salt, oregano, ground cumin, ground cloves and ground cinnamon
1 clove garlic, crushed
750 g/1¾ lb rump steak, cut into 2.5 cm/1 inch cubes
freshly ground pepper
250 g/8 oz button mushrooms

AMERICAN

4 tablespoons oil
1 small onion, peeled and chopped
4 tablespoons red wine vinegar
½ teaspoon each salt, oregano, ground cumin, ground cloves and ground cinnamon
1 clove garlic, crushed
1¾ lb top round steak, cut into 1 inch cubes
freshly ground pepper
2 cups button mushrooms

Heat 2 × 15 ml spoons/2 tablespoons of the oil in a saucepan. Add the onion and sauté until golden brown. Stir in the vinegar, salt, oregano, spices and garlic. Cover and simmer for 15 to 20 minutes, then allow to cool. Lay the meat cubes in a dish, brush with the remaining oil and sprinkle with pepper. When the basting sauce has cooled, pour over the steak and leave in the refrigerator to marinate for 2 to 4 hours.

Thread the steak cubes on to skewers alternately with the mushrooms. Brush with the marinade and cook over hot glowing charcoal, or under a hot grill (broiler), for 12 to 15 minutes for rare steak, 20 minutes for well done. Turn and baste frequently with the marinade. Serve with baked potatoes, a tossed green salad, and courgette and tomato kebabs.

SERVES 6 TO 8

Gingered Beef

METRIC/IMPERIAL

750 g/1½ lb rump, boneless sirloin or good blade steak, cut 4 cm/1½ inches thick
120 ml/4 fl oz soy sauce
2 × 5 ml spoons/2 tablespoons vegetable oil
3 × 5 ml spoons/3 tablespoons honey
1 clove garlic, crushed
1 × 15 ml spoon/1 tablespoon grated root ginger

AMERICAN

1½ lb top round steak, boneless sirloin or good blade steak, cut 1½ inches thick
½ cup soy sauce
2 tablespoons vegetable oil
3 tablespoons honey
1 clove garlic, crushed
1 tablespoon grated ginger root

Slice the meat across the grain into 5 mm (¼ inch) strips and place in a bowl. Mix the remaining ingredients and pour over, turning the meat about to coat evenly. Leave to marinate for 1 hour, turning the meat several times. Remove the meat strips from the marinade and thread on to skewers, concertina or 'snake' fashion. Cook under a very hot grill (broiler) for about 3 minutes, turning once and brushing with the marinade. The meat should be rare on the inside. Serve inside buttered bread rolls with chopped celery or beansprouts.

SERVES 4 TO 6

Chinese Smoked Meatballs

METRIC/IMPERIAL

4 dried Chinese mushrooms
1 small can water chestnuts, drained, rinsed and finely chopped
450 g/1 lb lean minced beef
2 × 15 ml spoons/2 tablespoons soy sauce
2 × 15 ml spoons/2 tablespoons cornflour
2 × 15 ml spoons/1 tablespoon finely chopped spring onion
1 × 15 ml spoon/1 tablespoon finely chopped root ginger
1 medium carrot, peeled and grated
1 × 15 ml spoon/1 tablespoon rice wine or dry sherry
1 × 5 ml spoon/1 teaspoon sesame oil

For smoking:

2 × 15 ml spoons/2 tablespoons brown sugar
2 × 15 ml spoons/2 tablespoons black tea leaves
2 × 15 ml spoons/2 tablespoons fennel seeds

To serve:

2 × 5 ml spoons/2 teaspoons sesame oil, mixed with 2 × 15 ml spoons/2 tablespoons soy sauce
2 spring onions, finely chopped

AMERICAN

4 dried Chinese mushrooms
1 small can water chestnuts, drained, rinsed and finely chopped
1 lb lean ground beef
2 tablespoons soy sauce
2 tablespoons cornstarch
1 tablespoon finely chopped scallion
1 tablespoon finely chopped ginger root
1 medium carrot, peeled and grated
1 tablespoon rice wine or dry sherry
1 teaspoon sesame oil

For smoking:

2 tablespoons brown sugar
2 tablespoons black tea leaves
2 tablespoons fennel seeds

To serve:

2 teaspoons sesame oil, mixed with 2 tablespoons soy sauce
2 scallions, finely chopped

Soak the mushrooms in hot water to cover for 15 minutes or until soft. Drain, remove stems and chop caps finely. Place them with the chestnuts in a large bowl, add the remaining ingredients and mix well by hand until the mixture is firm and compact. Shape into walnut-size balls and arrange in one layer on a greased wire rack or Chinese bamboo steamer. Cover and steam over boiling water in a wok or deep frying pan (skillet) for 15 minutes.

To smoke the meatballs, you need an old frying pan (skillet), wok or other metal container, lined with aluminium foil. Combine brown sugar, tea leaves and fennel seeds and place in the bottom. Set over high heat and when the mixture starts to smoke, put the rack containing the meatballs over the smoke. Cover tightly with a lid or aluminium foil and leave for another 5 minutes, then turn heat off and leave meatballs for a further 10 minutes, still covered. To serve, brush the meatballs with a little of the sesame-soy mixture and sprinkle with spring onions (scallions). Serve remaining sesame-soy mixture separately, for dipping. Serve with plain boiled rice and beansprouts.

SERVES 4

Italian Lamb Stew

METRIC/IMPERIAL
1 kg/2 lb boneless lamb, cut from leg or shoulder
2 × 15 ml spoons/2 tablespoons oil
250 g/8 oz bacon, diced
1 onion, peeled and sliced
2 cloves garlic, crushed
salt
freshly ground pepper
1 × 5 ml spoon/1 teaspoon chopped fresh marjoram or 1 × 2.5 ml spoon/½ teaspoon dried marjoram
1 × 5 ml spoon/1 teaspoon chopped fresh rosemary or 1 × 1.5 ml spoon/¼ teaspoon dried rosemary
120 ml/4 fl oz red wine
2 × 15 ml spoons/2 tablespoons tomato purée
extra 2 × 15 ml spoons/2 tablespoons red wine

AMERICAN
2 lb boneless lamb, cut from leg or shoulder
2 tablespoons oil
½ lb bacon, diced
1 onion, peeled and sliced
2 cloves garlic, crushed
salt
freshly ground pepper
1 teaspoon chopped fresh marjoram or ½ teaspoon dried marjoram
1 teaspoon chopped fresh rosemary or ¼ teaspoon dried rosemary
½ cup red wine
2 tablespoons tomato paste
extra 2 tablespoons red wine

Trim excess fat from the meat and cut into bite-size squares. Heat the oil in a large heavy frying pan (skillet). Add the bacon, onion and garlic and sauté until golden. Remove with a slotted spoon and set aside. Add half the meat and brown on all sides, then remove from the pan and repeat with the remaining meat. Return the meat to the pan and season with salt, pepper, marjoram and rosemary. Stir in the red wine and cook gently until the wine reduces to half its original quantity. Add the bacon mixture, tomato purée (paste) and enough water to cover the meat. Cover and simmer slowly for about 1½ hours or until tender. Add the 2 tablespoons red wine just before serving for extra flavour. Serve with flat ribbon noodles or fluffy boiled rice and a crisp green salad.
SERVES 4 TO 6

Italian Lamb Stew

Red-Cooked Lamb

METRIC/IMPERIAL	AMERICAN
1.5 kg/2–3 lb boned shoulder of lamb, cubed	*2–3 lb boneless lamb for stew, cubed*
salt	*salt*
pepper	*pepper*
2 × 15 ml spoons/2 tablespoons oil	*2 tablespoons oil*
1 onion, peeled and chopped	*1 onion, peeled and chopped*
1 clove garlic, crushed	*1 clove garlic, crushed*
3 × 15 ml spoons/3 tablespoons soy sauce	*3 tablespoons soy sauce*
4 × 15 ml spoons/4 tablespoons dry sherry	*¼ cup dry sherry*
2 × 5 ml spoons/2 teaspoons sugar	*2 teaspoons sugar*
120 ml/¼ pint brown stock	*⅔ cup brown stock*
2 slices root ginger	*2 slices ginger root*
2 bay leaves	*2 bay leaves*
2 × 5 ml spoons/2 teaspoons cornflour	*2 teaspoons cornstarch*
1 small red pepper, cored, seeded and cut into strips	*1 small red pepper, seeded and cut into strips*

Season the meat well. Heat the oil in a frying pan (skillet), brown the meat and sauté the onion and garlic until transparent. Drain and transfer to an ovenproof dish or casserole. Mix together the soy sauce, sherry, sugar and stock. Pour over the meat and mix well. Add the ginger and bay leaves. Cook in a moderate oven (180°C/350°F, Gas Mark 4) for 1½ to 2 hours, or until the meat is tender; 30 minutes before serving, stir in the cornflour (cornstarch), blended with 2 tablespoons cold water. Just before serving, remove the ginger and bay leaves, and sprinkle with red pepper. Serve with plain boiled rice.

SERVES 4 TO 6

Honey-Ginger Lamb

METRIC/IMPERIAL	AMERICAN
1 boned shoulder of lamb, rolled	*1 boned and rolled shoulder of lamb for stew*
175 g/6 oz warmed honey	*½ cup warmed honey*
2 × 15 ml spoons/2 tablespoons lemon juice	*2 tablespoons lemon juice*
1 × 15 ml spoon/1 tablespoon soy sauce	*1 tablespoon soy sauce*
1 × 1.25 ml spoon/¼ teaspoon ground cloves	*¼ teaspoon ground cloves*
1 × 5 ml spoon/1 teaspoon ground ginger	*1 teaspoon ground ginger*
stock or vegetable water for gravy	*stock or vegetable water for gravy*

Weigh the meat to calculate the required cooking time. Lamb should be roasted for 25 minutes per 450 g/1 lb, plus 25 minutes extra. Roast the meat in a preheated hot oven (220°C/425°F, Gas Mark 7) for the first 20 minutes. Meanwhile, mix the warmed honey, lemon juice, soy sauce, cloves and ginger, then baste the meat with the mixture. Turn the oven down to moderate (180°C/350°F, Gas Mark 4) and roast meat for the remaining required time, basting and turning it frequently. Place the meat on a serving dish. Skim the pan juices and add stock or vegetable water to make a gravy.

SERVES 4 TO 6

Korma Lamb

METRIC/IMPERIAL	AMERICAN
4 shallots, peeled	*4 shallots, peeled*
3 cloves garlic, peeled	*3 cloves garlic, peeled*
6 kemiri (candlenuts)	*6 kemiri (candlenuts)*
450 ml/¾ pint thick coconut milk (see page 92)	*2 cups thick coconut milk* (see page 92)
450 g/1¼ lb boned leg of lamb, cubed	*1¼ lb boneless lamb for stew, cubed*
salt	*salt*
3 × 15 ml spoons/3 tablespoons vegetable oil	*3 tablespoons vegetable oil*
1 small onion, peeled and finely sliced	*1 small onion, peeled and finely sliced*
1½ × 5 ml spoons/1½ teaspoons ground coriander	*1½ teaspoons ground coriander*
1 × 2.5 ml spoon/½ teaspoon ground cumin	*½ teaspoon ground cumin*
1 × 5 ml spoon/1 teaspoon ground ginger	*1 teaspoon ground ginger*
4 whole cloves	*4 whole cloves*
2.5 cm/1 inch piece cinnamon stick	*1 inch piece cinnamon stick*
3 whole cardamoms	*3 whole cardamoms*
1 salam leaf (or bay leaf)	*1 salam leaf (or bay leaf)*
1 sereh stalk, bruised, or 1 × 2.5 ml spoon/½ teaspoon ground sereh (or dried lemon grass)	*1 sereh stalk, bruised, or ½ teaspoon ground sereh (or dried lemon grass)*
3 × 15 ml spoons/3 tablespoons tamarind water (see *Fried Mackerel with Tamarind Sauce*, Fish chapter)	*3 tablespoons tamarind water* (see *Fried Mackerel with Tamarind Sauce*, Fish chapter)
1 × 2.5 ml spoon/½ teaspoon freshly ground white pepper	*½ teaspoon freshly ground white pepper*

Mince (grind) the shallots, garlic and kemiri (candlenuts), then transfer to a blender or food processor, add 2 × 15 ml spoons/2 tablespoons coconut milk and work to a smooth paste. Put the mixture in a bowl, add the lamb and a little salt and mix well. Leave to marinate for 30 minutes. Heat the oil in a pan, add the onion and sauté gently until soft. Add the spices, salam leaf (or bay leaf) and sereh (or dried lemon grass). Stir-fry for a few seconds, then add the meat and marinade and fry for 2 minutes. Add the tamarind water, and salt and pepper to taste. Cover and cook gently for 15 minutes, stirring every 5 minutes to prevent burning. Stir in the remaining coconut milk and simmer for 40 minutes or until the meat is tender and the sauce is quite thick. Discard the salam leaf (or bay leaf), sereh stalk, if using, cloves, cinnamon stick and cardamoms. Taste and adjust the seasoning. Serve hot.

SERVES 4

Red-Cooked Lamb

福

Lamb Provençal

METRIC/IMPERIAL	AMERICAN
450 g/1 lb boned leg of lamb	*1 lb boneless leg of lamb*
2 × 15 ml spoons/2 tablespoons vegetable oil	*2 tablespoons vegetable oil*
1 onion, peeled and sliced	*1 onion, peeled and sliced*
1 clove garlic, crushed	*1 clove garlic, crushed*
1 × 397 g/14 oz can tomatoes	*1 can (16 oz) tomatoes*
1 × 15 ml spoon/1 tablespoon tomato purée	*1 tablespoon tomato paste*
150 ml/¼ pint dry white wine	*⅔ cup dry white wine*
1 sprig rosemary	*1 sprig rosemary*
1 sprig thyme	*1 sprig thyme*
1 bay leaf	*1 bay leaf*
salt	*salt*
freshly ground black pepper	*freshly ground black pepper*
100 g/4 oz sliced mushrooms	*1 cup sliced mushrooms*
1 green pepper, cored, seeded and sliced	*1 green pepper, seeded and sliced*

Trim any excess fat from the lamb and cut into 2.5 cm/1 inch cubes. Heat the oil in a flameproof casserole or heavy-based pan. Add the onion and garlic and saute until golden. Add the lamb cubes and cook, stirring frequently, for 5 minutes or until evenly browned. Stir in the tomatoes and their juice, tomato puree (paste) and wine. Add the herbs and salt and pepper to taste. Stir well, then cover and simmer for 45 minutes. Add the sliced mushrooms and green pepper to the casserole. Check the seasoning, cover and continue simmering for a further 20 minutes. Discard the herbs and serve with brown rice.

SERVES 4

Pork Chops with Orange

METRIC/IMPERIAL	AMERICAN
1 clove garlic	*1 clove garlic*
2 × 5 ml spoons/2 teaspoons chopped fresh parsley	*2 teaspoons chopped fresh parsley*
2 × 5 ml spoons/2 teaspoons ground fennel	*2 teaspoons ground fennel*
salt and pepper	*salt and pepper*
4 pork chops	*4 center cut pork chops*
2 × 15 ml spoons/2 tablespoons oil	*2 tablespoons oil*
125 ml/¼ pint fresh orange juice	*⅔ cup fresh orange juice*
3 × 15 ml spoons/3 tablespoons white wine	*3 tablespoons white wine*
2 × 5 ml spoons/2 teaspoons cornflour blended with 2 × 15 ml spoons/2 tablespoons cold water	*2 teaspoons cornstarch, blended with 2 tablespoons cold water*
1 orange	*1 orange*
watercress to garnish	*watercress to garnish*

Rub the garlic, herbs and seasoning into the chops. Heat the oil in a frying pan (skillet) and brown the chops on both sides. Transfer to a casserole and add the orange juice and wine. Cook in a preheated moderate oven (180°C/350°F, Gas Mark 4) for 45 minutes to 1 hour. After 25 minutes stir in the blended cornflour (cornstarch). Remove the skin and pith from the orange and cut into 4 thick slices. Place 1 slice on each chop and baste with sauce. Serve hot.

SERVES 4

Spanish Pork with Pineapple

METRIC/IMPERIAL
50 g/2 oz lard
1.5 kg/3 lb lean boneless pork, cut into 3.5 cm/1½ inch cubes
1 × 15 ml spoon/1 tablespoon sugar
3 × 15 ml spoons/3 tablespoons flour
salt
freshly ground black pepper
2 onions, peeled and chopped
450–750 ml/¾–¼ pints beef stock
1 × 5 ml spoon/1 teaspoon coriander seeds, soaked in 2 × 15 ml spoons/2 tablespoons warm water
1 clove garlic, chopped
1 × 5 ml spoon/1 teaspoon crushed chilli chipotle (or other chilli pepper)
2 tomatoes, peeled, seeded and coarsely chopped
225 g/8 oz fresh pineapple, peeled, cored and coarsely chopped
2 medium yams or sweet potatoes, peeled and diced

AMERICAN
¼ cup lard
3 lb lean boneless pork, cut into 1½ inch cubes
1 tablespoon sugar
3 tablespoons flour
salt
freshly ground black pepper
2 onions, peeled and chopped
2–3 cups beef stock
1 teaspoon coriander seeds, soaked in 2 tablespoons warm water
1 clove garlic, chopped
1 teaspoon crushed chili chipotle (or other chili pepper)
2 tomatoes, peeled, seeded and coarsely chopped
½ lb fresh pineapple, peeled, cored and coarsely chopped
2 medium yams or sweet potatoes, peeled and diced

Heat the lard in a heavy frying pan (skillet) and sauté the pork, turning frequently, until browned on all sides. Transfer to a large flameproof casserole, using a slotted spoon. Sprinkle with sugar and cook, stirring constantly, over a very low heat for 3 to 5 minutes, or until the sugar dissolves completely. Add the flour, salt and pepper to taste and cook, stirring, for 5 minutes. Remove from the heat. Add the onions to the fat remaining in the frying pan (skillet) and sauté until transparent and soft, but not brown. Add the stock, stirring well to scrape any sediment from the bottom of the pan, and bring to the boil. Lower the heat.

Strain the liquor from the coriander seeds and mix the liquor with the garlic and crushed chilli, then add to the pan. Add the tomatoes and cook for 5 minutes, stirring to blend. Pour over the pork cubes and bring to the boil. Cover and bake in a preheated moderate oven (180°C/350°F, Gas Mark 4) for 1½ to 2 hours or until tender.

Using a slotted spoon, remove the meat and set aside. Strain the gravy into a large container and skim off excess fat. Return the meat to the casserole and add the gravy with the remaining ingredients. Return to the oven for 20 to 25 minutes, until the fruit and vegetables are tender.

SERVES 6

Spanish Pork with Pineapple

Hungarian Pork

METRIC/IMPERIAL
25 g/1 oz lard
750 g/1½ lb boned leg of pork, cubed
1 large onion, peeled and chopped
1 clove garlic, finely chopped
1 × 15 ml spoon/1 tablespoon paprika
1 × 2.5 ml spoon/½ teaspoon caraway seeds
1 × 2.5 ml spoon/1 teaspoon cayenne
salt
pepper
large pinch dried thyme
large pinch dried marjoram
100 g/4 oz button mushrooms
2 red peppers, cored, seeded and sliced
150 ml/¼ pint white stock
2 × 5 ml spoons/2 teaspoons cornflour, blended with 2 × 15 ml spoons/2 tablespoons cold water
150 ml/¼ pint soured cream
chopped parsley to garnish

AMERICAN
2 tablespoons lard
1½ lb boneless leg of pork, cubed
1 large onion, peeled and chopped
1 clove garlic, finely chopped
1 tablespoon paprika
½ teaspoon caraway seeds
1 teaspoon cayenne
salt
pepper
large pinch dried thyme
large pinch dried marjoram
1 cup button mushrooms
2 red peppers, seeded and sliced
⅔ cup white stock
2 teaspoons cornstarch, blended with 2 tablespoons cold water
⅔ cup sour cream
chopped parsley to garnish

Heat the lard in a heavy frying pan (skillet) and lightly brown the meat, onion and garlic. Stir in all the seasonings and herbs. Place the mushrooms and red peppers in the bottom of a casserole and add the meat mixture and stock. Cook in a moderate oven (180°C/350°F, Gas Mark 4) for about 1½ hours or until the meat is tender. Half an hour before serving, stir in the blended cornflour (cornstarch). Just before serving, pour in the soured cream and garnish with parsley.

SERVES 4 TO 6

Italian Pork Chops with Fennel

METRIC/IMPERIAL
2 large bulbs fennel, trimmed and chopped
3 juniper berries, crushed
4 large pork chops
salt
freshly ground pepper
2 × 15 ml spoons/2 tablespoons olive oil

AMERICAN
2 large bulbs fennel, trimmed and chopped
3 juniper berries, crushed
4 large center cut pork chops
salt
freshly ground pepper
2 tablespoons olive oil

Mix the fennel and juniper berries together and put a layer of this mixture in the base of a flat flameproof dish. Lay the pork chops on top, season with salt and pepper to taste and sprinkle the remaining fennel mixture over the top. Spoon over the oil, cover and refrigerate for at least 4 hours, basting occasionally. Heat the grill (broiler), uncover the dish and place the chops in the dish under the grill (broiler). Cook the chops for 12 to 15 minutes each side, turning them over frequently, until cooked through.

SERVES 4

Pork Vindaloo

METRIC/IMPERIAL

1 × 2.5 ml spoon/$\frac{1}{2}$ teaspoon cardamom seeds
1 × 2.5 ml spoon/$\frac{1}{2}$ teaspoon ground cloves
1 × 2.5 ml spoon/$\frac{1}{2}$ teaspoon ground ginger
1 × 15 ml spoon/1 tablespoon ground coriander
2 × 5 ml spoons/2 teaspoons turmeric
4 × 5 ml spoons/4 teaspoons ground chilli
1 × 5 ml spoon/1 teaspoon ground cumin
1 × 5 ml spoon/1 teaspoon salt
1 × 2.5 ml spoon/$\frac{1}{2}$ teaspoon freshly ground black pepper
200 ml/$\frac{1}{3}$ pint vinegar
450 g/1 lb boned pork, cut into 4 cm/$1\frac{1}{2}$ inch cubes
50 g/2 oz ghee or clarified butter
5 cloves garlic, sliced

AMERICAN

$\frac{1}{2}$ teaspoon cardamom seeds
$\frac{1}{2}$ teaspoon ground cloves
$\frac{1}{2}$ teaspoon ground ginger
1 tablespoon ground coriander
2 teaspoons ground turmeric
4 teaspoons ground chili
1 teaspoon ground cumin
1 teaspoon salt
$\frac{1}{2}$ teaspoon freshly ground black pepper
$\frac{7}{8}$ cup vinegar
1 lb boneless pork, cut into $1\frac{1}{2}$ inch cubes
$\frac{1}{4}$ cup ghee or clarified butter
5 cloves garlic, sliced

Mix the spices and seasonings to a thick paste with a little of the vinegar, then rub into the pork. Melt the ghee or clarified butter in a heavy frying pan (skillet), add the garlic and sauté for 1 to 2 minutes, stirring frequently. Add the pork to the pan and cover with the remaining vinegar. Bring to the boil, then lower the heat, cover and simmer for about 1 hour or until the meat is tender. Serve hot with chappattis and plenty of plain yogurt.

SERVES 4

Breast of Veal Samarkand

METRIC/IMPERIAL

1.5 kg/3 lb breast of veal
3 × 15 ml spoons/3 tablespoons oil
3 × 15 ml spoons/3 tablespoons flour
3 × 15 ml spoons/3 tablespoons dry sherry
100 g/4 oz sultanas
1 × 15 ml spoon/1 tablespoon tomato purée
350 ml/12 fl oz beef stock (or canned consommé or stock cubes and water)
2 × 15 ml spoons/2 tablespoons redcurrant jelly
1 × 5 ml spoon/1 teaspoon salt
pinch cayenne
2 × 5 ml spoons/2 teaspoons ground cumin
250 ml/8 fl oz soured cream
chopped parsley to garnish

AMERICAN

3 lb breast of veal
3 tablespoons oil
3 tablespoons flour
3 tablespoons dry sherry
1 cup golden raisins
1 tablespoon tomato paste
$1\frac{1}{2}$ cups beef stock (or canned consommé or bouillon cubes and water)
2 tablespoons redcurrant jelly
1 teaspoon salt
pinch cayenne
2 teaspoons ground cumin
1 cup sour cream
chopped parsley to garnish

Remove the meat from the bones and cut into bite-size squares. Heat the oil in a wide heavy saucepan and quickly brown the meat on all sides. Sprinkle the flour over the meat and cook gently for a few minutes, stirring. Pour the sherry into the pan and stir well, scraping up any brown bits from the bottom. Add the sultanas (golden raisins) and tomato purée (paste) and mix in, then pour in the stock. Bring the mixture to the boil and add the redcurrant jelly, salt, cayenne and cumin. Cover the pan tightly, turn the heat down, and simmer gently for 1 hour or until the veal is tender. Stir in the soured cream and heat through. Taste and adjust the seasoning. Spoon into a heated serving bowl and serve garnished with chopped parsley, and tiny new potatoes steamed in their jackets.

SERVES 6 TO 8

Mediterranean-Style Veal Chops

METRIC/IMPERIAL

25 g/1 oz butter
1 tablespoon oil
4 veal chops
salt
freshly ground black pepper
350 g/12 oz mushrooms, sliced
2 large green or red peppers, cored, seeded and sliced
350 g/12 oz tomatoes, peeled and sliced
1 tablespoon chopped fresh basil
1 teaspoon sugar
300 ml/$\frac{1}{2}$ pint chicken stock or water
lemon wedges to garnish

AMERICAN

2 tablespoons butter
1 tablespoon oil
4 veal chops
salt
freshly ground black pepper
$\frac{3}{4}$ lb mushrooms, sliced
2 large green or red peppers, seeded and sliced
$\frac{3}{4}$ lb tomatoes, peeled and sliced
1 tablespoon chopped fresh basil
1 teaspoon sugar
$1\frac{1}{4}$ cups chicken stock or water
lemon wedges to garnish

Melt the butter and oil together in a frying pan (skillet) and fry the chops quickly until browned on both sides. Season and remove from pan. Fry the prepared mushrooms and peppers until soft, add the tomatoes, seasoning, basil, sugar and stock or water. Boil for 3 minutes. Return chops to the pan and simmer, uncovered, for about 30 minutes. The sauce should be very thick. Arrange the chops on a heated dish with the sauce and garnish with lemon wedges.

SERVES 4

Breast of Veal Samarkand;
Mediterranean-Style Veal Chops

Liver and Onions

METRIC/IMPERIAL
4 × 15 ml spoons/4 tablespoons olive oil
350 g/12 oz onions, peeled and thinly sliced
1 × 15 ml spoon/1 tablespoon fresh sage or ¼ teaspoon dried sage
salt
freshly ground black pepper
400–450 g/14 oz–1 lb calf's or lamb's liver, very thinly sliced and veins removed
1 × 15 ml spoon/1 tablespoon wine vinegar
1 × 15 ml spoon/1 tablespoon water
To garnish:
2 × 15 ml spoons/2 tablespoons chopped fresh chives or parsley

AMERICAN
4 tablespoons olive oil
¾ lb onions, peeled and thinly sliced
1 tablespoon fresh sage or ¼ teaspoon dried sage
salt
freshly ground black pepper
14 oz–1 lb calf's or lamb's liver, very thinly sliced and veins removed
1 tablespoon wine vinegar
1 tablespoon water
To garnish:
2 tablespoons chopped fresh chives or parsley

Heat 2 × 15 ml spoons/2 tablespoons of the oil in a large, heavy-based frying pan (skillet). When hot, put in the onions and cook over a low heat, stirring frequently, for 15 to 20 minutes, until the onions are soft and golden. Stir in the sage and a little salt and pepper, then spread the mixture over the base of a hot serving dish. Keep hot.

While the onions are cooking, pat each slice of liver dry with kitchen paper and cut into pieces roughly 4 cm/1½ inches square. Using kitchen paper towels, wipe clean the pan (skillet) in which the onions were cooked. Pour the remaining oil into the pan and, when sizzling hot, put in the pieces of liver and fry briskly, turning frequently, for 2 to 3 minutes, until the liver changes colour on the outside but is still juicy inside. Add salt and pepper and pile the liver on top of the onions. Add the vinegar and water to the pan (skillet), boil for a few seconds, stirring and scraping up the juices from the base of the pan, and pour over the liver. Sprinkle with chopped chives or parsley.

SERVES 4

Loin of Veal with Rosemary

METRIC/IMPERIAL
1 × 2.5 kg/5 lb loin of veal
salt
freshly ground black pepper
2 × 15 ml spoons/2 tablespoons crumbled fresh rosemary or 1 × 15 ml spoon/1 tablespoon dried rosemary
75 g/3 oz butter, softened
250 ml/8 fl oz dry white wine

AMERICAN
5 lb loin of veal
salt
freshly ground black pepper
2 tablespoons crumbled fresh rosemary or 1 tablespoon dried rosemary
6 tablespoons butter, softened
1 cup dry white wine

Ask your butcher to bone and trim the veal. Season generously with salt and pepper, then rub on both sides with the rosemary and butter. Roll up and tie into a neat shape with white string. Place in a roasting pan, pour over the wine, and roast in a moderate oven (180°C/350°F, Gas Mark 4), allowing 30 minutes per 450 g (1 lb) or until cooked to your liking. Baste with the pan juices every 20 minutes. Remove the string and serve cut in slices with the juices poured over.

SERVES 6

Peachy Sausages

METRIC/IMPERIAL
1 kg/2 lb thick sausages
1 × 15 ml spoon/1 tablespoon oil
1 × 15 ml spoon/1 tablespoon vinegar
120 ml/4 fl oz peach juice
4 × 15 ml spoons/4 tablespoons tomato sauce
1 × 15 ml spoon/1 tablespoon brown sugar
1 × 15 ml spoon/1 tablespoon grated onion
1 × 2.5 ml spoon/½ teaspoon Worcestershire sauce
1 × 1.5 ml spoon/¼ teaspoon salt
2 × 5 ml spoons/2 teaspoons chopped fresh oregano or 1 × 2.5 ml spoon/½ teaspoon dried oregano
dash of Tabasco or chilli sauce
summer savory to garnish

AMERICAN
2 lb thick sausages
1 tablespoon oil
1 tablespoon vinegar
½ cup peach nectar
¼ cup tomato sauce
1 tablespoon brown sugar
1 tablespoon grated onion
½ teaspoon Worcestershire sauce
¼ teaspoon salt
2 teaspoons chopped fresh oregano or ½ teaspoon dried oregano
dash of hot pepper sauce
summer savory to garnish

Prick the sausages in several places, place in a frying pan (skillet) with water to cover and simmer for 5 minutes, then drain. Parboiled in this way, the sausages will cook through without scorching or bursting. Place the remaining ingredients in a saucepan and simmer for 5 minutes, stirring now and again. Pour over the sausages and allow to stand for 30 minutes. Cook the sausages under the grill until crisp and brown on all sides, brushing frequently with the glaze. Spoon remaining glaze over the sausage and garnish with summer savory to serve.

SERVES 6 TO 8

Liver and Onions

Poultry & Game

Chicken with Cucumber in Sesame Sauce

METRIC/IMPERIAL

8 chicken fillets (boned, skinless breasts)
2 spring onions
2 slices root ginger, peeled
750 ml/1¼ pints water
2 small cucumbers
Sesame sauce:
1 × 5 ml spoon/1 teaspoon finely chopped spring onion
2 × 5 ml spoons/2 tablespoons sesame paste or crunchy peanut butter
1 × 15 ml spoon/1 tablespoon light soy sauce
1 × 1.25 ml spoon/¼ teaspoon dry mustard
3 × 15 ml spoons/3 tablespoons water
1 × 5 ml spoon/1 teaspoon salt
1 × 5 ml spoon/1 teaspoon chilli oil (or 1 × 5 ml spoon/1 teaspoon peanut oil with a dash of Tabasco sauce
To garnish:
spring onion brushes
salad burnet

AMERICAN

8 chicken fillets (boned, skinless breasts
2 scallions
2 slices ginger root, peeled
3 cups water
2 small cucumbers
Sesame sauce:
1 teaspoon finely chopped scallion
2 tablespoons sesame paste or crunchy peanut butter
1 tablespoon light soy sauce
¼ teaspoon dry mustard
3 tablespoons water
1 teaspoon salt
1 teaspoon chili oil (or 1 teaspoon peanut oil with a dash of hot pepper sauce)
To garnish:
scallion brushes
salad burnet

Place the chicken fillets in a saucepan with the spring onions (scallions), ginger and water. Bring to the boil, reduce the heat, cover the pan and simmer gently for 6 minutes. Allow to cool in the stock, then remove and cut into short strips (the size of matchsticks). Peel the cucumbers, leaving a few strips of green skin for colour, then halve them and scoop out the seeds with a teaspoon. Cut the cucumber into strips the same size as the chicken. Cover the chicken and cucumber with plastic wrap and refrigerate until needed. Place all the ingredients for the sesame sauce in a small bowl and mix well to combine. Arrange the chicken on one side of a dish, and the cucumber next to it. Garnish with spring onion (scallion) brushes and salad burnet. Just before serving, spoon a little sauce over the chicken and cucumber and serve at once as a main course or as part of a cold buffet.

SERVES 4

Lemon Chicken

METRIC/IMPERIAL

1 × 1.5 kg/3 lb oven-ready chicken with giblets
salt
1 medium onion, peeled
1 small bay leaf
1 lemon
1 carrot, peeled and quartered
2 celery sticks, chopped
1 × 15 ml spoon/1 tablespoon fresh marjoram or 1 × 5 ml spoon/1 teaspoon dried marjoram
4 black peppercorns
600 ml/1 pint water
Sauce:
450 ml/¾ pint hot stock strained from the chicken
40 g/1½ oz butter
40 g/1½ oz plain flour
1 egg yolk
4 × 15 ml spoons/4 tablespoons single cream
juice of ½ lemon
sprigs of parsley to garnish

AMERICAN

1 × 3 lb roasting chicken with giblets
salt
1 medium onion, peeled
1 small bay leaf
1 lemon
1 carrot, peeled and quartered
2 celery sticks, chopped
1 tablespoon fresh marjoram or 1 teaspoon dried marjoram
4 black peppercorns
2½ cups water
Sauce:
2 cups hot stock strained from the chicken
3 tablespoons butter
⅓ cup all-purpose flour
1 egg yolk
4 tablespoons light cream
juice of ½ lemon
sprigs of parsley to garnish

Sprinkle the body cavity of the chicken with salt and insert the onion and the bay leaf. Cut the lemon in half, rub one cut surface over the chicken and reserve the other half for garnishing. Place the bird in a deep pan with a tight fitting lid. Add the washed giblets, a thin strip of lemon rind, the carrot, celery, marjoram, peppercorns, 1 teaspoon salt and the water. Bring to the boil, cover the pan tightly and simmer gently for about 1 hour, or until the chicken is tender and the juices run clear when the bird is pierced with a skewer.

Strain the stock from the chicken, leaving the bird in the pan to keep warm. Melt the butter in a small saucepan, remove from the heat, stir in the flour and cook gently, stirring, for 2 minutes. Gradually add the hot stock, stirring briskly until smoothly blended. Return the pan to the heat and cook, stirring continuously, until the sauce boils, then simmer gently for 5–10 minutes until it has thickened.

Mix the egg yolk with the cream, stir in 2 tablespoons of the hot sauce, then pour into the sauce and stir over low heat for 1 minute, but do not boil. Add lemon juice to taste and adjust the seasoning. To serve, carve the chicken into joints, arrange on a serving dish and spoon over the sauce. Garnish with the reserved lemon half cut into wedges and sprigs of parsley and serve with rice.

SERVES 4 TO 6

Tarragon Chicken en Cocotte; Lemon Chicken

Tarragon Chicken en Cocotte

METRIC/IMPERIAL

1 × 1.5 kg/3 lb oven-ready chicken
salt
freshly ground black pepper
50 g/2 oz butter
8 sprigs fresh tarragon or 1 × 5 ml spoon/1 teaspoon dried tarragon
1 × 15 ml spoon/1 tablespoon oil
1 onion, peeled and sliced
1 carrot, peeled and sliced
1 stick celery, sliced
450 ml/¾ pint chicken stock
1 × 15 ml spoon/1 tablespoon cornflour
2 × 15 ml spoons/2 tablespoons medium sherry
2 × 15 ml spoons/2 tablespoons chopped fresh tarragon or parsley
sprig of tarragon to garnish

AMERICAN

1 × 3 lb roasting chicken
salt
freshly ground black pepper
¼ cup butter
8 sprigs fresh tarragon or 1 teaspoon dried tarragon
1 tablespoon oil
1 onion, peeled and sliced
1 carrot, peeled and sliced
1 celery stalk, sliced
2 cups chicken stock
1 tablespoon cornstarch
2 tablespoons cream sherry
2 tablespoons chopped fresh tarragon or parsley
sprig of tarragon to garnish

Rinse the chicken under running cold water, drain and pat dry with kitchen paper towels. Season the body cavity with salt and pepper and insert 15 g/½ oz/1 tablespoon of the butter and half of the sprigs of dried tarragon. Truss the bird if necessary. Heat the oil and remaining butter in a flameproof casserole. Place the chicken breast-down in the dish and adjust the heat so that the chicken browns in 3 to 5 minutes but the fat is not hot enough to discolour. Turn the chicken at intervals to brown the sides and then the back; this gentle browning process takes a total of 10 to 15 minutes.

Lift the chicken on to a plate. Add the onion, carrot and celery to the pan and sauté gently in the same fat for 5 minutes. Sprinkle with a little salt and pepper and add the rest of the tarragon. Replace the bird on top of the vegetables and cover with aluminium foil and a lid. Transfer to a preheated oven (180°C/350°F, Gas Mark 4) and cook for 1 hour 20 minutes. Pierce the thickest part of the thigh with a metal skewer and if the juices run clear the bird is cooked.

Place the chicken on a hot serving dish, discard any trussing strings and keep hot. Add the stock to the pan and boil for a few minutes, stirring to free any sediment from the base of the pan. Skim off any surface fat. Stir in the cornflour (cornstarch) blended with the sherry and bring to the boil. Stir until the sauce thickens slightly. Adjust the seasoning, strain the sauce into a hot sauce boat and stir in the chopped herbs. Immediately before serving, garnish the breast of the bird with a sprig of tarragon and spoon over a little of the sauce.

SERVES 4 TO 6

Sesame Chicken with Rice

METRIC/IMPERIAL	AMERICAN
50 g/2 oz flour	*½ cup flour*
1 × 15 ml spoon/1 tablespoon sesame seeds	*1 tablespoon sesame seeds*
¾ × 5 ml spoon/¾ teaspoon ground ginger	*¾ teaspoon ground ginger*
salt	*salt*
pepper	*pepper*
1.5 kg/3 lb oven-ready chicken, jointed, or 4 chicken quarters	*3 lb roasting chicken, jointed, or 4 chicken quarters*
50 g/2 oz butter	*¼ cup butter*
1 × 15 ml spoon/1 tablespoon oil	*1 tablespoon oil*
300 ml/½ pint stock	*1¼ cups stock*
4 × 15 ml spoons/4 tablespoons dry white wine	*¼ cup dry white wine*
150 g/6 oz long grain rice	*1 cup long grain rice*
1 × 2.5 ml spoon/½ teaspoon ground coriander	*½ teaspoon ground coriander*
pinch chilli powder	*pinch chili powder*
chopped parsley to garnish	*chopped parsley to garnish*

Mix together the flour, sesame seeds, two-thirds of the ginger, and salt and pepper to taste. Coat chicken pieces with the mixture and fry till golden in the butter and oil in a frying pan (skillet). Drain on kitchen paper towels and place in a casserole. Blend the remaining flour mixture with the fat left in the pan, add the stock and wine, bring to the boil and cook to thicken. Pour over the chicken and cook in a cool oven (150°C/300°F, Gas Mark 3) for 1½ to 2 hours. Put the rice in a saucepan with 600 ml (1 pint) cold water and 1 × 5 ml spoon (1 teaspoon) salt. Bring to the boil, stir, then simmer, covered, for 10 to 12 minutes until tender. Drain rice and rinse with boiling water. Mix with the remaining ginger and seasonings. Pile on a serving dish, arrange the chicken on top and garnish with parsley.

SERVES 4

Herbed Chicken

METRIC/IMPERIAL	AMERICAN
1 × 1.75 kg/4 lb oven-ready chicken	*1 × 4 lb roasting chicken*
1 × 15 ml spoon/1 tablespoon oil	*1 tablespoon oil*
3 × 15 ml spoons/3 tablespoons lemon juice	*3 tablespoons lemon juice*
salt	*salt*
freshly ground black pepper	*freshly ground black pepper*
1 × 397 g/14 oz can tomatoes	*1 can (16 oz) tomatoes*
1 × 5 ml spoon/1 teaspoon chopped fresh marjoram	*1 teaspoon chopped fresh marjoram*
1 × 5 ml spoon/1 teaspoon chopped fresh parsley	*1 teaspoon chopped fresh parsley*
1 × 5 ml spoon/1 teaspoon snipped chives	*1 teaspoon chopped chives*
1 × 5 ml spoon/1 teaspoon chopped fresh thyme	*1 teaspoon chopped fresh thyme*

Put the chicken in a roasting pan, brush with the oil and lemon juice, then sprinkle with salt and pepper. Roast in a preheated moderately hot oven (190°C/375°F, Gas Mark 5) for 45 minutes. Mix together the tomatoes, herbs, and salt and pepper to taste, then pour over the chicken. Reduce the oven temperature to moderate (180°C/350°F, Gas Mark 4) and continue roasting for 45 minutes, basting the chicken frequently with the tomato mixture. Serve hot.

SERVES 4 TO 6

Chicken Mussalam

METRIC/IMPERIAL	AMERICAN
1.5 kg/3 lb chicken, skinned and cut into 8 pieces	*3 lb chicken, skinned and cut into 8 pieces*
175 ml/6 fl oz natural yogurt	*¾ cup natural yogurt*
1 large onion, peeled and chopped	*1 large onion, peeled and chopped*
3 cloves garlic, sliced	*3 cloves garlic, sliced*
3 green chillis	*3 green chilis*
1 × 5 ml spoon/1 teaspoon ground coriander	*1 teaspoon ground coriander*
175 g/6 oz ghee or clarified butter	*¾ cup ghee or clarified butter*
2.5 cm/1 inch piece cinnamon stick	*1 inch piece cinnamon stick*
10 whole cardamoms	*10 whole cardamoms*
10 whole cloves	*10 whole cloves*
1 × 5 ml spoon/1 teaspoon ground ginger	*1 teaspoon ground ginger*
1 × 5 ml spoon/1 teaspoon salt	*1 teaspoon salt*
1 × 5 ml spoon/1 teaspoon freshly ground black pepper	*1 teaspoon freshly ground black pepper*
1 × 2.5 ml spoon/½ teaspoon saffron, soaked in 1 × 15 ml spoon/1 tablespoon boiling water for 30 minutes	*½ teaspoon saffron, soaked in 1 tablespoon boiling water for 30 minutes*

Make 3 deep cuts in each piece of chicken with a sharp knife. Work the yogurt, onion, garlic, chillis and coriander in a blender or food processor, then pour over the chicken. Cover, place in refrigerator and leave to marinate overnight. Drain the chicken, reserving the marinade. Melt the ghee or clarified butter in a flameproof casserole, add the chicken and fry for about 15 minutes until browned on all sides. Add the spices and seasonings, except the saffron, and fry for a further 3 minutes, stirring constantly. Add the saffron with its liquid, then add the reserved marinade. Cover the casserole and cook in a preheated moderately hot oven (190°C/375°F, Gas Mark 5) for about 30 minutes or until the chicken is tender and the sauce is very thick. Serve hot.

SERVES 4

Pheasant in Cream and Brandy Sauce

METRIC/IMPERIAL

2 pheasants, plucked, drawn and trussed
25 g/1 oz butter
1 × 15 ml spoon/1 tablespoon oil
2 × 15 ml spoons/2 tablespoons brandy
2 onions, peeled and finely chopped
2 carrots, peeled and finely chopped
1 bay leaf
1 sprig fresh thyme
300 ml/½ pint double cream
salt
freshly ground black pepper
To garnish:
bunch watercress
sorrel leaves

AMERICAN

2 pheasants, plucked, drawn and trussed
2 tablespoons butter
1 tablespoon oil
2 tablespoons brandy
2 onions, peeled and finely chopped
2 carrots, peeled and finely chopped
1 bay leaf
1 sprig fresh thyme
1¼ cups heavy cream
salt
freshly ground black pepper
To garnish:
bunch watercress
sorrel leaves

Wipe the pheasants inside and out with kitchen paper towels. Put the butter and oil in a flameproof casserole and heat gently until the butter has melted. Brown the pheasants quickly on all sides. Warm the brandy, pour it over the pheasants and ignite. When the flames have died down, add the onions, carrots, bay leaf and thyme, cover with a lid and cook over a low heat for about 1 hour, or until the pheasants are tender when pierced with a skewer. Remove the bay leaf, stir in the cream, mix well and bring briefly to the boil. Remove from the heat, taste for seasoning. Arrange the whole birds on a warmed serving platter, garnished with watercress and sorrel, and serve the sauce separately.
SERVES 4–6

Pheasant in Cream and Brandy Sauce

Spiced Duck in Coconut Milk

METRIC/IMPERIAL

100 g/4 oz ghee or clarified butter
1.75 kg/4 lb oven-ready duck, skinned and cut up into 8 pieces
1 large onion, peeled and sliced
2 cloves garlic, sliced
1 × 5 ml spoon/1 teaspoon chilli powder
1 × 5 ml spoon/1 teaspoon ground ginger
2 × 5 ml spoons/2 teaspoons ground cumin
1 × 5 ml spoon/1 teaspoon ground coriander
1 × 15 ml spoon/1 tablespoon Garam Masala (see below)
1 × 5 ml spoon/1 teaspoon salt
150 ml/$\frac{1}{4}$ pint vinegar
300 ml/$\frac{1}{2}$ pint coconut milk (see page 92)

AMERICAN

$\frac{1}{2}$ cup ghee or clarified butter
4 lb oven-ready duck, skinned and cut up into 8 pieces
1 large onion, peeled and sliced
2 cloves garlic, sliced
1 teaspoon chili powder
1 teaspoon ground ginger
2 teaspoons ground cumin
1 teaspoon ground coriander
1 1 tablespoon Garam Masala (see below)
1 teaspoon salt
$\frac{2}{3}$ cup vinegar
$1\frac{1}{4}$ cups coconut milk (see page 92)

Melt the ghee or clarified butter in a heavy pan or flameproof casserole, add the duck and fry until browned on all sides, then remove. Add the onion and garlic to the pan and fry gently until soft. Mix the spices and salt to a paste with 3 × 15 ml spoons/3 tablespoons of the vinegar, then add to the pan and fry for a further 3 minutes, stirring constantly. Stir in the remaining vinegar and the coconut milk, then return the duck to the pan. Cover and simmer for 45 minutes. Serve hot.
SERVES 4

Garam Masala

Use either 15 ml spoons/tablespoons or 5 ml spoons/teaspoons to measure.

$1\frac{1}{2}$ spoons whole cardamoms
5 spoons coriander seeds
1 spoon cumin seeds
$1\frac{1}{2}$ spoons whole cloves
6 spoons black peppercorns

Remove the seeds from the cardamoms and place on a baking sheet with the other ingredients. Bake in a preheated very hot oven (240°C/475°F, Gas Mark 9) for 10 minutes, then leave to cool. Grind to a fine powder with a pestle and mortar, coffee mill, blender or food processor. Store in an airtight jar.

Timbales of Duck

METRIC/IMPERIAL
3 slices fresh brown bread, crusts removed, and made into crumbs
150 ml/¼ pint milk
225 g/8 oz cooked duck trimmings, roughly chopped
2 × 15 ml spoons/2 tablespoons sherry
1 small onion, peeled and quartered
1 × 15 ml spoon/1 tablespoon sprigs parsley
salt
freshly ground black pepper
grated nutmeg
ground cloves
3 egg whites
sprigs watercress to garnish
sauce Valoise (sauce Béarnaise with 1 × 5 ml spoon/1 teaspoon beef extract added) to serve

AMERICAN
3 slices fresh brown bread, crusts removed, and made into crumbs
⅔ cup milk
½ lb cooked duck trimmings, roughly chopped
2 tablespoons sherry
1 small onion, peeled and quartered
1 tablespoon sprigs parsley
salt
freshly ground black pepper
grated nutmeg
ground cloves
3 egg whites
sprigs watercress to garnish
sauce Valoise (sauce Béarnaise with 1 teaspoon beef extract added) to serve

Place the breadcrumbs in a small pan, add the milk and cook very gently until most of the milk has been absorbed. Mix together the duck, sherry, onion and parsley. Add the bread mixture, and salt and pepper, nutmeg and cloves to taste. Work in a blender or food processor until smooth. Adjust the seasoning and place the mixture in a large bowl. Whisk the egg whites until stiff but not dry and fold into the meat mixture. Divide between 4 buttered individual moulds, leaving room for the mixture to rise. Stand in a baking tin (pan) half filled with hot water. Bake in a moderate oven (180°C/350°F, Gas Mark 4) for 30 minutes. Allow to stand for a few minutes before unmoulding on to a heated serving dish. Garnish with watercress and serve with creamed spinach, potato croquettes and sauce Valoise.
SERVES 4

Casserole of Hare

METRIC/IMPERIAL
1 hare, skinned and jointed
½ bottle dry white wine or dry cider
6 black peppercorns
6 whole cloves
1 × 2.5 ml spoon/½ teaspoon grated nutmeg
1 × 2.5 ml spoon/½ teaspoon salt
2 cloves garlic, crushed
1 bay leaf
3 × 15 ml spoons/3 tablespoons beef dripping or lard
3 onions, peeled and thinly sliced

AMERICAN
1 hare, skinned and jointed
½ bottle dry white wine or dry cider
6 black peppercorns
6 whole cloves
½ teaspoon grated nutmeg
½ teaspoon salt
2 cloves garlic, crushed
1 bay leaf
3 tablespoons beef dripping or lard
3 onions, peeled and thinly sliced

Casserole of Hare

Place the pieces of hare in a shallow dish. Mix the wine or cider with the spices, salt, garlic and bay leaf and pour over the hare. Cover and leave to marinate in a cool place for 3 hours, or overnight. Drain the hare, reserving the marinade, and dry thoroughly on kitchen paper towels. Heat the dripping or lard in a frying pan (skillet) and brown the hare pieces on all sides. Transfer to a casserole. Sauté the onions in the fat remaining in the pan (skillet) until they start to soften; transfer to the casserole. Pour in the reserved marinade. Cook in a preheated moderate oven (160°C/325°F, Gas Mark 3) for 2½ to 3 hours, or until the hare is tender.
SERVES 4

Pot-Roasted Venison

METRIC/IMPERIAL
2.25 kg/5 lb boneless venison roast
75 g/3 oz butter
1 large carrot, peeled and finely chopped
1 leek, trimmed and finely chopped
250 ml/8 fl oz beef stock
salt
freshly ground black pepper
250 ml/8 fl oz soured cream
Marinade:
120 ml/4 fl oz olive oil
3 cloves garlic, crushed
1 medium onion, peeled and sliced
3 whole cloves
1 bay leaf
1 × 15 ml spoon/1 tablespoon salt
1 × 15 ml spoon/1 tablespoon ground peppercorns
1 × 5 ml spoon/1 teaspoon dried thyme
1 × 5 ml spoon/1 teaspoon allspice or juniper berries
2 slices root ginger, peeled and chopped
4 sprigs parsley
sufficient red wine to cover meat

AMERICAN
5 lb boneless venison roast
6 tablespoons butter
1 large carrot, peeled and finely chopped
1 leek, trimmed and finely chopped
1 cup beef stock
salt
freshly ground black pepper
1 cup sour cream
Marinade:
½ cup olive oil
3 cloves garlic, crushed
1 medium onion, peeled and sliced
3 whole cloves
1 bay leaf
1 tablespoon salt
1 tablespoon ground peppercorns
1 teaspoon dried thyme
1 teaspoon allspice or juniper berries
2 slices ginger root, peeled and chopped
4 sprigs parsley
sufficient red wine to cover meat

Place the venison in a deep crockery or plastic bowl. Combine all marinade ingredients and pour over the venison. Cover and leave in the refrigerator for 3 days, turning now and again. Remove the venison from the marinade and pat dry with kitchen paper towels. Strain the marinade and set aside 450 ml/¾ pint/2 cups. Heat the butter in a large, heavy flameproof casserole or Dutch oven and slowly brown the venison on all sides. Add the carrot, leek, reserved marinade and the beef stock. Season with salt and pepper to taste, cover tightly, and cook in a preheated moderate oven (160°C/325°F, Gas Mark 3) for 1½ hours or until the venison is tender.

Remove the meat to a platter and keep warm in the turned-off oven with the door open. Reduce liquid left in casserole by rapid boiling until it measures about 350 ml/12 fl oz/1½ cups. Strain into a small, clean saucepan, stir in the soured cream and heat through (but do not boil). Taste for seasoning and serve as a sauce with the venison.
SERVES 8

Vegetables & Salads

Fennel and Lemon Salad

METRIC/IMPERIAL
1 large bulb fennel
handful of parsley, washed and well dried
1 × 15 ml spoon/1 tablespoon lemon juice
2 × 15 ml spoons/2 tablespoons olive or groundnut oil
1 × 5 ml spoon/1 teaspoon sugar (optional)
2 × 15 ml spoons/2 tablespoons double cream
salt
freshly ground black pepper
1 lemon

AMERICAN
1 large bulb fennel
handful of parsley, washed and well dried
1 tablespoon lemon juice
2 tablespoons olive or peanut oil
1 teaspoon sugar (optional)
2 tablespoons heavy cream
salt
freshly ground black pepper
1 lemon

Wash and trim the fennel, if necessary, then cut into short thin strips of matchstick size. Soak the fennel in very cold water for a few minutes, then drain and dry. Finely chop the parsley. Beat together the lemon juice, oil, sugar if used, cream, and salt and pepper to taste, or blend in a blender or food processor. Peel rind from lemon, cut away pith. Slice lemon into thin slices and cut each slice into quarters. Combine fennel, lemon and parsley and toss in the dressing. Serve with roast pork or veal.
SERVES 4

Mushrooms with Oregano

METRIC/IMPERIAL
750 g/1½ lb mushrooms
7 × 15 ml spoons/7 tablespoons oil
2 cloves garlic, crushed
2 × 15 ml spoons/2 tablespoons chopped oregano (or any other fresh herb)
salt
freshly ground pepper
pinch grated nutmeg

AMERICAN
1½ lb mushrooms
7 tablespoons oil
2 cloves garlic, crushed
2 tablespoons chopped oregano (or any other fresh herb)
salt
freshly ground pepper
pinch grated nutmeg

Wipe over the mushrooms with a damp cloth and trim the stalks, then slice. Heat the oil in a large frying pan (skillet) over a fairly high heat; sauté the mushrooms, a few at a time. As they brown remove them to a plate and add more fresh ones. When all the mushrooms are browned return to the pan, reduce the heat and add the garlic and oregano, season with salt and pepper to taste and grated nutmeg. Cook gently for about 2 minutes, stirring occasionally. Spoon into a heated serving dish. Served with hot buttered toast as a light luncheon dish.
SERVES 6

Cucumber Sesame Salad

METRIC/IMPERIAL
3 cucumbers, peeled and thinly sliced
120 ml/4 fl oz cider vinegar
2 × 15 ml spoons/2 tablespoons salt
120 ml/4 fl oz whipping or double cream, chilled
120 ml/4 fl oz thick coconut cream (see page 92)
1 × 15 ml spoon/1 tablespoon sugar
1 × 15 ml spoon/1 tablespoon sesame oil
2 × 15 ml spoons/2 tablespoons snipped chives
1 × 15 ml spoon/1 tablespoon toasted sesame seeds
1 × 15 ml spoon/1 tablespoon chopped fresh parsley

AMERICAN
3 cucumbers, peeled and thinly sliced
½ cup cider vinegar
2 tablespoons salt
½ cup heavy cream, chilled
½ cup thick coconut cream (see page 92)
1 tablespoon sugar
1 tablespoon sesame oil
2 tablespoons chopped chives
1 tablespoon toasted sesame seeds
1 tablespoon chopped fresh parsley

Cover the cucumber with vinegar and salt and leave to marinate for 1 hour. Drain and transfer to a serving bowl. Whip cream until it forms soft peaks and fold in coconut cream, sugar, sesame oil and chives. Pour over the cucumber and sprinkle with sesame seeds and chopped parsley.
SERVES 4

Avocado, Grapefruit and Sesame Salad

METRIC/IMPERIAL
2 large avocados
juice 1 small lemon
2 grapefruit, peel and pith removed and divided into segments
1 × 15 ml spoon/1 tablespoon chopped mint
1 small lettuce
2 × 15 ml spoons/2 tablespoons sesame seeds
sprigs mint to garnish

AMERICAN
2 large avocados
juice 1 small lemon
2 grapefruit, peel and pith removed and divided into segments
1 tablespoon chopped mint
1 small head of lettuce
2 tablespoons sesame seeds
sprigs mint to garnish

Peel the avocados, cut in half lengthwise, then remove the stones (seeds). Slice the pulp, place in a bowl, then sprinkle with the lemon juice. Fold in the grapefruit and chopped mint. Arrange the lettuce leaves in individual serving bowls. Divide the salad between them, then sprinkle with the sesame seeds. Garnish with mint sprigs and serve immediately.
SERVES 4

Feta Salad

Feta Salad

METRIC/IMPERIAL
4 tomatoes, quartered
1 large cucumber, peeled and sliced
1 medium onion, thinly sliced
100 g/4 oz feta cheese, broken into chunks
12–16 soft black olives
4 × 15 ml spoons/4 tablespoons olive oil
2 × 15 ml spoons/2 tablespoons lemon juice
1 clove garlic, crushed
salt and black pepper
1 × 15 ml spoon/1 tablespoon thinly chopped fresh basil and oregano

AMERICAN
4 tomatoes, quartered
1 large cucumber, peeled and sliced
1 medium onion, thinly sliced
$\frac{2}{3}$ cup feta cheese, broken into chunks
12–16 soft black olives
$\frac{1}{4}$ cup olive oil
2 tablespoons lemon juice
1 clove garlic, crushed
salt and black pepper
1 tablespoon thinly chopped fresh basil and oregano

Place the tomatoes, cucumber, onion, cheese and olives in a bowl. Combine the oil, lemon juice, garlic, salt, pepper and herbs in a screw top jar. Shake until the mixture is pale and smooth, then pour over the salad. Toss well and serve.
SERVES 4 TO 6

Tomatoes with Basil

METRIC/IMPERIAL
4–5 large ripe tomatoes
$\frac{1}{2}$ Spanish onion
5–6 large basil leaves
1–2 × 15 ml spoons/1–2 tablespoons olive oil
salt
freshly ground pepper
squeeze lemon juice

AMERICAN
4–5 large ripe tomatoes
$\frac{1}{2}$ Bermuda or Spanish onion
5–6 large basil leaves
1–2 tablespoons olive oil
salt
freshly ground pepper
squeeze lemon juice

Peel the tomatoes, remove the cores and cut into wedges. Finely slice the onion. Shred the basil leaves, but do not chop as they tend to bruise. Combine the tomatoes, onion and basil in a bowl. Drizzle over a little oil, season with salt to taste, a fresh grinding of pepper and a squeeze of lemon juice. Toss lightly.
SERVES 4

Cucumber and Tomato Raita

METRIC/IMPERIAL	AMERICAN
1 small or ½ large cucumber, sliced	*1 small or ½ large cucumber, sliced*
1 × 2.5 ml spoon/½ teaspoon salt	*½ teaspoon salt*
4 tomatoes, thinly sliced	*4 tomatoes, thinly sliced*
300 ml/½ pint natural yogurt	*1¼ cups natural yogurt*
2 × 15 ml spoons/2 tablespoons chopped mint	*2 tablespoons chopped mint*
freshly ground white pepper	*freshly ground white pepper*
sprig mint to garnish	*sprig mint to garnish*

Put the cucumber in a sieve (strainer), sprinkle with the salt and leave to drain for 30 minutes to draw out the moisture. Arrange the cucumber and tomatoes in a serving dish. Mix the yogurt with the chopped mint and pepper to taste, then pour over the salad. Garnish with mint. Serve chilled.

SERVES 4

Cucumber and Tomato Raita; Italian Salad

Italian Salad

METRIC/IMPERIAL	AMERICAN
½ curly endive, separated into leaves	*½ head chicory, separated into leaves*
1 head chicory, sliced into rings	*1 head endive, sliced into rings*
1 bulb fennel, sliced into rings	*1 bulb fennel, sliced into rings*
1 small head radiccio, separated into leaves	*1 small head red chicory, separated into leaves*
8 radishes, sliced if large	*8 radishes, sliced if large*
4 × 15 ml spoons/4 tablespoons vinaigrette dressing	*¼ cup vinaigrette dressing*
salt	*salt*
freshly ground black pepper	*freshly ground black pepper*
sprig of fennel	*sprig of fennel*

Put all the ingredients in a salad bowl, toss well, then taste and adjust the seasoning. Garnish with fennel.

SERVES 4

Ratatouille

METRIC/IMPERIAL
1 large aubergine, sliced
salt
4 × 15 ml spoons/4 tablespoons olive oil
2 medium onions, peeled and thinly sliced
1 clove garlic, crushed
750 g/1½ lb ripe tomatoes, peeled, seeded and quartered
1 × 2.5 ml spoon/½ teaspoon dried oregano
450 g/1 lb courgettes, sliced
1 large green pepper, cored, seeded and thinly sliced
1 large red pepper, cored, seeded and thinly sliced
freshly ground black pepper
freshly chopped parsley to garnish

AMERICAN
1 large eggplant, sliced
salt
¼ cup olive oil
2 medium onions, peeled and thinly sliced
1 clove garlic, crushed
1½ lb ripe tomatoes, peeled, seeded and quartered
½ teaspoon dried oregano
1 lb zucchini, sliced
1 large green pepper, seeded and thinly sliced
1 large red pepper, seeded and thinly sliced
freshly ground black pepper
freshly chopped parsley to garnish

Sprinkle the aubergine (eggplant) slices with salt and leave to drain for 30 minutes in a colander. Wash and dry well with kitchen paper towels. Heat the oil in a large saucepan, add the onions, garlic, tomatoes and oregano and cook gently for 3 to 4 minutes until the juices flow from the tomatoes. Add the remaining vegetables, and salt and pepper to taste. Stir well. Bring to the boil, stirring constantly, then lower the heat, cover with a lid and cook gently, stirring occasionally, for at least 30 minutes or until the vegetables are soft. Remove from the heat, taste for seasoning and serve, garnished with parsley, hot as a vegetable dish or chilled as a starter.
SERVES 4 TO 6

Marinated Mushrooms

METRIC/IMPERIAL
450 g/1 lb small button mushrooms, thinly sliced
120 ml/4 fl oz olive oil
4 × 15 ml spoons/4 tablespoons lemon juice
1–2 cloves garlic, thinly sliced
1 bay leaf
1 × 15 ml spoon/1 tablespoon chopped fresh parsley
8–10 large sprigs fresh thyme
salt
freshly ground black pepper
1 × 5 ml spoon/1 teaspoon French mustard
1 × 2.5 ml spoon/½ teaspoon caster sugar

AMERICAN
1 lb small button mushrooms, thinly sliced
½ cup olive oil
¼ cup lemon juice
1–2 cloves garlic, thinly sliced
1 bay leaf
1 tablespoon chopped fresh parsley
8–10 large sprigs fresh thyme
salt
freshly ground black pepper
1 teaspoon Dijon-style mustard
½ teaspoon sugar

Put the sliced mushrooms into a bowl. Mix all the remaining ingredients together in a small bowl and mix well. Pour the marinade over the mushrooms and mix well. Cover and refrigerate for about 4 hours, stirring occasionally. Spoon into a serving dish and serve chilled with garlic and herb French bread.
SERVES 4 TO 6

Leeks à la Grecque

METRIC/IMPERIAL
6 young leeks
1 × 15 ml spoon/1 tablespoon chopped fresh tarragon or 1 × 5 ml spoon/1 teaspoon dried tarragon
4 × 5 ml spoons/4 teaspoons lemon juice
1 clove garlic, crushed
1 × 15 ml spoon/1 tablespoon chopped fresh parsley
1 tomato, peeled and seeded
pinch dried thyme
salt
freshly ground pepper
1 bay leaf
4 × 15 ml spoons/4 tablespoons olive oil
250 ml/8 fl oz water

AMERICAN
6 young leeks
1 tablespoon chopped fresh tarragon or 1 teaspoon dried tarragon
4 teaspoons lemon juice
1 clove garlic, crushed
1 tablespoon chopped fresh parsley
1 tomato, peeled and seeded
pinch dried thyme
salt
freshly ground pepper
1 bay leaf
¼ cup olive oil
1 cup water

Trim the root ends of leeks and remove any coarse outer leaves, as only the white part and a little of the green of leeks are edible. Slit the leeks right down one side and wash thoroughly under running cold water to remove any grit. Place the trimmed leeks in a heavy saucepan large enough to take them whole. Add the remaining ingredients. Cover the pan and bring to the boil. Reduce heat and simmer for 8 to 10 minutes. Allow to cool, then chill if to be eaten cold.
SERVES 6

Variations:

Leeks in Wine Prepare the leeks as above but use 250 ml/8 fl oz/1 cup of red wine instead of the tomato and water.

Green Beans à la Grecque Substitute 750 g/1½ lb young French (green) beans for the leeks. Wash, top and tail, but leave whole. Cook as above.

Mushrooms à la Grecque Use 450 g/1 lb button mushrooms. Carefully wash, then trim and cook as above.

Brussels Sprouts with Caraway Seeds

METRIC/IMPERIAL
750 g/1½ lb Brussels sprouts
chicken stock
15 g/½ oz butter
1 × 2.5 ml spoon/½ teaspoon salt
freshly ground black pepper
2 × 5 ml spoons/2 teaspoons caraway seeds

AMERICAN
1½ lb Brussels sprouts
chicken stock
1 tablespoon butter
½ teaspoon salt
freshly ground black pepper
2 teaspoons caraway seeds

Wash the Brussels sprouts, trim off the tough outer leaves and cut a small cross in the bottom of each. Pour chicken stock to a depth of 2.5 cm/1 inch in a saucepan. Bring the stock to the boil and add the sprouts. Return to the boil and simmer, uncovered, for 5 minutes. Cover and cook for 6 to 10 minutes longer, or until just tender. Drain if necessary. Add the remaining ingredients, toss lightly and serve at once.
SERVES 6

Mexican-style Cauliflower

METRIC/IMPERIAL	AMERICAN
1 medium cauliflower	1 medium cauliflower
3 tomatoes, peeled, seeded and chopped	3 tomatoes, peeled, seeded and chopped
2 × 15 ml spoons/2 tablespoons chopped fresh parsley	2 tablespoons chopped fresh parsley
pinch dried cloves	pinch dried cloves
1 × 1.25 ml spoon/¼ teaspoon ground cinnamon	¼ teaspoon ground cinnamon
1 × 15 ml spoon/1 tablespoon capers	1 tablespoon capers
2 × 15 ml spoons/2 tablespoons chopped olives	2 tablespoons chopped olives
3 × 15 ml spoons/3 tablespoons grated cheese	3 tablespoons grated cheese
2 × 15 ml spoons/2 tablespoons fine breadcrumbs	2 tablespoons fine bread crumbs
1 × 15 ml spoon/1 tablespoon olive or salad oil	1 tablespoon olive or salad oil

Trim the cauliflower and divide into florets. Cook the florets, covered, in a small amount of boiling salted water until barely tender. Drain. Mix the tomatoes, parsley, cloves, cinnamon, capers and olives and heat gently to make a sauce. Pour a little of the sauce into an ovenproof serving dish, add the cauliflower and cover with the remaining sauce. Sprinkle with the cheese, breadcrumbs and oil and bake until brown in a preheated hot oven (220°C/425°F, Gas Mark 7) for about 20 minutes.

SERVES 6

Courgette (Zucchini) Medley

METRIC/IMPERIAL	AMERICAN
1 large onion, peeled and sliced	1 large onion, peeled and sliced
1 clove garlic, crushed	1 clove garlic, crushed
2 × 15 ml spoons/2 tablespoons olive oil	2 tablespoons olive oil
large pinch salt	large pinch salt
freshly ground black pepper	freshly ground black pepper
3 × 15 ml spoons/3 tablespoons chopped fresh parsley	3 tablespoons chopped fresh parsley
1 × 5 ml spoon/1 teaspoon chopped fresh thyme or sage	1 teaspoon chopped fresh thyme or sage
450 g/1 lb French beans	1 lb green beans
450 g/1 lb courgettes	1 lb zucchini
4 large tomatoes, quartered	4 large tomatoes, quartered
4 tablespoons water	¼ cup water

Sauté the onion and garlic in the oil in a frying pan (skillet). Season with salt and pepper to taste and add the herbs. Cut the beans into lengths, and the courgettes (zucchini) into chunks. Add the beans, courgettes (zucchini), tomatoes and water to the pan and simmer, covered, for 10 minutes or until just tender. Serve as a vegetable or as a light lunch topped with grated cheese.

SERVES 4

Lentils with Tomatoes; Dhal

Dhal

METRIC/IMPERIAL
225 g/8 oz red lentils
600 ml/1 pint water
1 bay leaf
salt
freshly ground black pepper
25 g/1 oz butter or margarine
1 × 15 ml spoon/1 tablespoon oil
1 onion, peeled and finely chopped
1 clove garlic, crushed
1 × 2.5 ml spoon/½ teaspoon ground ginger or 1 × 5 ml spoon/1 teaspoon grated root ginger
1 × 2.5 ml spoon/½ teaspoon ground coriander
1 × 2.5 ml spoon/½ teaspoon ground cumin

AMERICAN
½ lb red lentils
2½ cups water
1 bay leaf
salt
freshly ground black pepper
2 tablespoons butter or margarine
1 tablespoon oil
1 onion, peeled and finely chopped
1 clove garlic, crushed
½ teaspoon ground ginger or 1 teaspoon grated ginger root
½ teaspoon ground coriander
½ teaspoon ground cumin

Place the lentils in a saucepan and add the water, bay leaf, salt and pepper. Cover the pan and bring to the boil. Simmer for 15 to 30 minutes until the lentils are swollen and the water has been absorbed to give a thickish purée. Heat the butter or margarine and oil in a clean pan and sauté the onion, garlic and ginger, if using, for 5 minutes until lightly browned. Add the rest of the spices and cook for 1 minute. Add the cooked lentil purée and cook gently for 5 minutes. Remove the bay leaf. Serve hot with rice or as an accompaniment to curry, or cold with a salad.
SERVES 4

Lentils with Tomatoes

METRIC/IMPERIAL
225 g/8 oz brown or green lentils
1 × 397 g/14 oz can tomatoes
600 ml/1 pint water
1 onion, peeled and chopped
1 × 15 ml spoon/1 tablespoon chopped fresh oregano, marjoram or basil, or 1 × 5 ml spoon/1 teaspoon dried mixed herbs
salt
freshly ground black pepper
1 × 15 ml spoon/1 tablespoon chopped fresh marjoram or parsley to garnish

AMERICAN
½ lb brown or green lentils
1 can (16 oz) tomatoes
2½ cups water
1 onion, peeled and chopped
1 tablespoon chopped fresh oregano, marjoram or basil, or 1 teaspoon dried mixed herbs
salt
freshly ground black pepper
1 tablespoon chopped fresh marjoram or parsley to garnish

Place the lentils in a saucepan. Pour in the tomatoes with the juice from the can and roughly cut up the tomatoes. Pour over the water and add the onion, herbs, and salt and pepper to taste. Cover the pan and bring to the boil. Then simmer gently for 1 to 1¼ hours until the lentils are tender and most of the liquid has evaporated, but the mixture is still moist. Stir occasionally towards the end of the cooking time to prevent the lentils from sticking. Serve hot, sprinkled with chopped marjoram or parsley as a vegetable accompaniment to grilled meats or chicken, or cold.
SERVES 4

White Bean Salad

METRIC/IMPERIAL	AMERICAN
225 g/8 oz dried white beans (mixture of haricot, butter beans, and black-eye peas)	*½ lb dried white beans (mixture of navy, butter beans, and black-eye peas)*
600 ml/1 pint water	*2½ cups water*
1 onion, peeled and chopped	*1 onion, peeled and chopped*
1 bay leaf	*1 bay leaf*
salt	*salt*
freshly ground black pepper	*freshly ground black pepper*
3 × 15 ml spoons/3 tablespoons olive oil	*3 tablespoons olive oil*
grated rind and juice 1 small lemon	*grated rind and juice 1 small lemon*
1 × 15 ml spoon/1 tablespoon capers	*1 tablespoon capers*
2 gherkins, sliced	*2 gherkins, sliced*
2 × 15 ml spoons/2 tablespoons chopped fresh parsley	*2 tablespoons chopped fresh parsley*
2 hard-boiled eggs, cut into wedges	*2 hard-cooked eggs, cut into wedges*
8 black olives	*8 black olives*

Soak the beans in the water overnight, or cover with 600 ml/1 pint/2½ cups boiling water and leave to soak for at least 2 hours. Drain the beans, reserve the liquid and make up to 600 ml/1 pint/2½ cups with water. Place the beans and the water in a saucepan and add the onion and bay leaf with salt and pepper. Cover the pan and bring the water to the boil. Simmer for 45 minutes to 1 hour until the beans are tender. Drain the beans and leave to cool thoroughly. To make the dressing, mix together the oil, lemon rind and juice, capers, gherkins, parsley, and salt and pepper. Pour half the dressing over the beans and leave to marinate for at least 30 minutes. Spoon the beans into a serving dish and arrange the hard-boiled (hard-cooked) eggs and olives on the top. Add the remaining dressing and serve.

SERVES 4

Beans with Cheese and Herbs

METRIC/IMPERIAL	AMERICAN
450 g/1 lb French beans	*1 lb green beans*
25 g/1 oz butter	*2 tablespoons butter*
1 × 15 ml spoon/1 tablespoon oil	*1 tablespoon oil*
2 × 15 ml spoons/2 tablespoons chopped fresh parsley or 1 × 5 ml spoon/1 teaspoon chopped fresh sage	*2 tablespoons chopped fresh parsley or 1 teaspoon chopped fresh sage*
1 clove garlic, crushed	*1 clove garlic, crushed*
salt	*salt*
freshly ground pepper	*freshly ground pepper*
good pinch grated nutmeg	*good pinch grated nutmeg*
2 × 15 ml spoons/2 tablespoons freshly grated Parmesan cheese	*2 tablespoons freshly grated Parmesan cheese*

Top and tail the beans. Leave whole if young, or cut in diagonal slices if larger. Cook in boiling salted water until just tender, then drain. Heat the butter and oil in a saucepan, stir in 1 × 15 ml/1 tablespoon of the chopped parsley or 1 × 2.5 ml spoon/½ teaspoon of the sage, and the garlic. Cook for 1 minute, stirring, then add the beans and season to taste with salt, pepper and nutmeg. Stir for another minute or two over a gentle heat until the beans are piping hot, then add the grated cheese and lightly stir through. Turn into a serving dish and sprinkle with remaining herbs. Serve with veal, pork or lamb.

SERVES 4

Catalan Broad Bean Casserole

METRIC/IMPERIAL	AMERICAN
100 g/4 oz lard	*½ cup lard*
225 g/8 oz bacon, diced	*½ lb bacon, diced*
225 g/8 oz butifarra or garlic sausage, sliced	*½ lb butifarra or garlic sausage, sliced*
1 onion, peeled and chopped	*1 onion, peeled and chopped*
2 cloves garlic, chopped	*2 cloves garlic, chopped*
2 tomatoes, peeled and chopped	*2 tomatoes, peeled and chopped*
bouquet garni (mint, thyme and parsley)	*bouquet garni (mint, thyme and parsley)*
few leaves summer savory	*few leaves summer savory*
1 × 5 ml spoon/1 teaspoon ground cinnamon	*1 teaspoon ground cinnamon*
2 cloves	*2 cloves*
2 kg/4½ lb broad beans, shelled	*4½ lb fava beans, shelled*
150 ml/¼ pint sweet red wine	*⅔ cup sweet red wine*
150 ml/¼ pint ham or chicken stock	*⅔ cup ham or chicken stock*
freshly ground black pepper	*freshly ground black pepper*
salt (as necessary)	*salt (as necessary)*

Heat the lard in a large flameproof casserole or heavy saucepan and fry the bacon and sausage until lightly coloured. Remove with a slotted spoon and reserve. Sauté the onion, garlic and tomatoes in the fat remaining in the pan until soft. Add the bouquet garni, summer savory and spices. Stir in the beans, bacon and sausage, then pour in the wine and stock. Season with pepper, and salt if necessary. Cover and cook over a low heat for about 30 minutes. Remove the bouquet garni. Serve hot, as a main dish.

SERVES 4

Spicy Tomato Salad

METRIC/IMPERIAL	AMERICAN
4 large, ripe tomatoes	*4 large, ripe tomatoes*
3 spring onions, including some green tops, finely chopped	*3 scallions, including some green tops, finely chopped*
1 × 15 ml spoon/1 tablespoon lime juice	*1 tablespoon lime juice*
¾ × 5 ml spoon/¾ teaspoon grated fresh ginger	*¾ teaspoon grated fresh ginger*
salt	*salt*
freshly ground pepper	*freshly ground pepper*

Cut the tomatoes crosswise into thin slices and arrange in overlapping circles on a platter. Sprinkle with the remaining ingredients, adding salt and pepper to taste. Serve at once.

SERVES 4

Sweetcorn with Tomato Sauce

Sweetcorn with Tomato Sauce

METRIC/IMPERIAL

450 g/1 lb frozen or canned sweetcorn kernels

Sauce:

50 g/2 oz lard

450 g/1 lb tomatoes, peeled and finely chopped, or 1 × 397 g/14 oz can tomatoes

4 cloves garlic, crushed

1 × 15 ml spoon/1 tablespoon paprika

1 × 2.5 ml spoon/½ teaspoon brown sugar

salt

freshly ground black pepper

dash of vinegar

4–6 × 15 ml spoons/4–6 tablespoons water

AMERICAN

1 lb frozen or canned whole kernel corn

Sauce:

¼ cup lard

1 lb tomatoes, peeled and finely chopped, or 1 can (16 oz) tomatoes

4 cloves garlic, crushed

1 tablespoon paprika

½ teaspoon brown sugar

salt

freshly ground black pepper

dash of vinegar

4–6 tablespoons water

Heat the lard in a saucepan and saute the tomatoes and garlic for 2 minutes, breaking the tomatoes down with a wooden spoon. Add the paprika, sugar, salt and pepper to taste, and the vinegar. Cook over a very low heat for about 15 minutes or until the mixture is reduced to a pulp. Meanwhile, cook the frozen sweetcorn in a little water until tender. If using canned sweetcorn, heat through. Drain the sweetcorn and transfer to a serving dish. Add just enough water to the tomato mixture to make a thick sauce. Spoon the tomato sauce over the sweetcorn and serve hot.

SERVES 4

Turkish Barley Salad

METRIC/IMPERIAL

200 g/7 oz barley

1 small cucumber, peeled, seeded and chopped

2 large ripe tomatoes, peeled, seeded and chopped

½ bunch radishes, trimmed and thinly sliced

15 g/½ oz chopped fresh parsley

2 × 15 ml spoons/2 tablespoons chopped fresh mint

4 spring onions, shredded into matchstick lengths

salt

freshly ground pepper

lettuce leaves to serve

Dressing:

3 × 15 ml spoons/3 tablespoons lemon juice

1 × 5 ml spoon/1 teaspoon salt

120 ml/4 oz olive oil

AMERICAN

1 cup barley

1 small cucumber, peeled, seeded and chopped

2 large ripe tomatoes, peeled, seeded and chopped

½ bunch radishes, trimmed and sliced

¼ cup chopped fresh parsley

2 tablespoons chopped fresh mint

4 scallions, shredded into matchstick lengths

salt

freshly ground pepper

lettuce leaves to serve

Dressing:

3 tablespoons lemon juice

1 teaspoon salt

½ cup olive oil

Cover the barley with cold water and bring to the boil. Remove from the heat, cover, and stand for 1 hour. Drain, cover again with salted cold water, bring to the boil and simmer until tender, 1 to 1½ hours. Meanwhile, make the dressing: put the lemon juice and salt into a bowl and gradually whisk in the oil. Drain the barley, and toss gently with the dressing. (This can be done ahead of time.) Toss the barley with the chilled vegetables and herbs and season with salt and pepper to taste. Serve on lettuce leaves.

SERVES 6

Accompaniments

Sauces and Stocks

As some of the recipes in the book require various stocks, the following are included regardless of their own herb content: fish stock, chicken stock, beef stock, white stock, brown stock. A bouquet garni, almost always used in stocks, is a bundle of any of 3 to 5 herbs tied together, such as parsley stalks, a bay leaf, a sprig of thyme, marjoram or oregano, and sometimes a small strip each of celery and leek.

For Bolognese sauce, see the recipe for *Tagliatelle alla Bolognese*, and for Béchamel sauce see the recipe for *Lasagne verde*.

Fish Stock
Place in a saucepan 450 g/1 lb fish heads and bones, 5 cups cold water, 1 cup dry white wine, 1 × 5 ml spoon/1 teaspoon peppercorns, 1 slice of onion, a few slices of carrot and a bouquet garni. Bring to the boil, skim the surface and then simmer, covered, for 15 minutes. Strain before using.

Chicken Stock
Place the following in a large saucepan: 450 g/1 lb chicken bones or pieces, 12 cups cold water, 1 sliced carrot, 1 sliced onion, 1 × 5 ml spoon/1 teaspoon peppercorns and a bouquet garni. Bring to the boil, skim surface, and simmer, covered, for 3 to 4 hours. Strain and chill. Lift off fat before using.

Beef Stock
Place the following in a large saucepan: 1 kg/2 lb beef bones, 450 g/1 lb chopped stewing beef, 1 each sliced carrot and onion, 12 cups cold water, 1 × 5 ml spoon/1 teaspoon peppercorns, 1 bouquet garni. Bring to the boil, skim the surface, then simmer, covered, for 4 to 5 hours. Strain and chill. Remove fat before using.

White stock
Use veal bones and veal in place of beef.

Brown Stock
Make this in the same way as beef stock but brown the bones and vegetables first. Place them in a greased roasting pan, sprinkle with a little oil, and roast in a hot oven (230°C/450°F, Gas Mark 8) until a rich brown, turning everything to brown evenly. Make sure to scrape up the brown bits from the roasting pan and add to the saucepan.

To Clarify Stock
Strain stock, chill and remove all fat. Heat gently with 1 crushed eggshell and 1 lightly beaten egg white for every 4 cups stock, whisking steadily until the mixture boils. Simmer undisturbed for 20 minutes. Line a colander with 2 layers of scalded muslin (cheesecloth) or disposable cloth, slide the egg white crust on to the cloth and slowly pour liquid through.

Savoury and herb butters

An effective garnish that adds extra flavour and succulence to plain grilled foods such as steaks, chops or fish. Savoury or herb butters make excellent 'toppings' for cooked vegetables and can be used to flavour stuffed hard-boiled (hard-cooked) eggs, to dress pasta or to enrich a plain soup.

For garnishing, chill the butters in the refrigerator and top each portion of food with a pat of butter immediately before serving. Savoury butters will keep in the refrigerator for up to 2 weeks, but herb butters are best used immediately.

Maître d'Hôtel Butter

METRIC/IMPERIAL	AMERICAN
100 g/4 oz unsalted butter, softened	*½ cup unsalted butter, softened*
2–3 × 15 ml spoons/2–3 tablespoons finely chopped fresh parsley	*2–3 tablespoons finely chopped fresh parsley*
2 × 5 ml spoons/2 teaspoons lemon juice	*2 teaspoons lemon juice*
salt	*salt*
freshly ground black pepper	*freshly ground black pepper*

Cream the butter until light and fluffy then beat in all the other ingredients. Turn on to greaseproof (waxed) paper, form into a 2.5 cm/1 inch diameter roll, wrap the paper around the roll, overwrap in aluminium foil and chill for several hours until firm. To use, cut into slices.

Variations:

Herb Butter
Add 1–2 × 15 ml spoons/1–2 tablespoons chopped fresh tarragon, mint or chives.

Orange Butter
Omit the parsley and add 1 × 15 ml spoon/¼ teaspoon ground coriander and a large pinch paprika.

Mustard Butter
Add 2 × 15 ml spoons/2 tablespoons French (Dijon-style) mustard.

Garlic Butter
Add 2 × 15 ml spoons/2 tablespoons finely grated shallot and 2 cloves garlic, finely crushed.

Anchovy Butter
Omit the salt and parsley. Add 6 to 8 canned anchovy fillets, previously drained and pounded to a paste.

Underground Pickle

METRIC/IMPERIAL	AMERICAN
450 g/1 lb carrots, peeled and cut up into sticks (about 3 cm × 5 mm/$1\frac{1}{4} \times \frac{1}{4}$ inch)	*1 lb carrots, peeled and cut up into sticks (about $1\frac{1}{4} \times \frac{1}{4}$ inch)*
225 g/8 oz parsnips, peeled and cut up into sticks (about 3 cm × 5 mm/$1\frac{1}{4} \times \frac{1}{4}$ inch)	*$\frac{1}{2}$ lb parsnips, peeled and cut up into sticks (about $1\frac{1}{4} \times \frac{1}{4}$ inch)*
225 g/8 oz turnips, peeled and cut up into 1 cm/$\frac{1}{2}$ inch square cubes	*$\frac{1}{2}$ lb turnips, peeled and cut up into $\frac{1}{2}$ inch square cubes*
225 g/8 oz celery, washed and cut into slices about 1 cm/$\frac{1}{2}$ inch thick	*$\frac{1}{2}$ lb celery, washed and cut up into slices about $\frac{1}{2}$ inch thick*
225 g/8 oz onions, peeled and sliced	*$\frac{1}{2}$ lb onions, peeled and sliced*
3 × 15 ml spoons/3 tablespoons salt	*3 tablespoons salt*
1 litre/$1\frac{3}{4}$ pints malt vinegar	*1 quart malt vinegar*
225 g/8 oz soft brown sugar	*$\frac{1}{2}$ lb firmly packed light brown sugar*
1 large clove garlic, crushed	*1 large clove garlic, crushed*
25 g/1 oz fresh ginger, peeled and thinly sliced	*1 oz fresh ginger, peeled and thinly sliced*
2 bay leaves	*2 bay leaves*
1 × 15 ml spoon/1 tablespoon mustard seeds	*1 tablespoon mustard seeds*
1 × 15 ml spoon/1 tablespoon fennel seeds	*1 tablespoon fennel seeds*
1 × 15 ml spoon/1 tablespoon allspice berries	*1 tablespoon allspice berries*
1 × 15 ml spoon/1 tablespoon black peppercorns	*1 tablespoon black peppercorns*

Place the vegetables in a large bowl, sprinkling each layer with the salt. Cover and leave for 12 hours to draw out the excess moisture. Rinse well to remove the salt, then drain and dry well. Place the vinegar in a large saucepan with the remaining ingredients. Heat slowly to dissolve the sugar, then bring to the boil and remove from the heat. Meanwhile, pack the vegetables loosely into prepared jars, allowing enough space for the vinegar and spices to surround all the vegetables. Pour in the hot vinegar and push the whole spices down the side of the jar. Seal the jars with airtight, vinegar-proof covers.
MAKES 2.5 kg/$5\frac{1}{2}$ lb

Pear and Ginger Chutney

METRIC/IMPERIAL	AMERICAN
25 g/1 oz root ginger, roughly chopped	*1 oz ginger root, roughly chopped*
1 × 5 ml spoon/1 teaspoon whole cloves	*1 teaspoon whole cloves*
2.75 kg/6 lb pears, peeled, cored and chopped	*6 lb pears, peeled, cored and chopped*
450 g/1 lb onions, peeled and chopped	*1 lb onions, peeled and chopped*
100 g/4 oz stem ginger, finely chopped	*$\frac{1}{4}$ lb preserved ginger, finely chopped*
grated rind and juice 3 oranges	*grated rind and juice 3 oranges*
750 g/$1\frac{1}{2}$ lb granulated sugar	*$1\frac{1}{2}$ lb sugar*
900 ml/$1\frac{1}{2}$ pints red wine vinegar	*$3\frac{3}{4}$ cups red wine vinegar*

Tie the root ginger and cloves in a muslin (cheesecloth) bag, then place all the ingredients in a large pan. Stir over a low heat until the sugar dissolves. Bring to the boil, reduce the heat and simmer for $1\frac{1}{2}$ hours or until the chutney is thick. Remove the muslin (cheesecloth) bag and spoon while still hot into prepared jars. Seal with airtight, vinegar-proof covers.
MAKES ABOUT 1.75 kg/4 lb

Underground Pickle

Horseradish Sauce with Walnuts

METRIC/IMPERIAL
2 × 15 ml spoons/2 tablespoons freshly grated horseradish
150 ml/$\frac{1}{4}$ pint soured cream
12 walnut halves, finely chopped
salt
freshly ground black pepper

AMERICAN
2 tablespoons freshly grated horseradish
$\frac{2}{3}$ cup sour cream
12 walnut halves, finely chopped
salt
freshly ground black pepper

Fold the freshly prepared horseradish into the soured cream with the nuts and salt and pepper to taste. Taste and add a little more horseradish if necessary. Serve with meats, especially beef, or fish such as mackerel.
MAKES ABOUT 300 ml/$\frac{1}{2}$ PINT/1$\frac{1}{4}$ CUPS

Pesto Sauce

METRIC/IMPERIAL
50 g/2 oz fresh basil leaves
3 cloves garlic, peeled
25 g/1 oz pine nuts
salt
25 g/1 oz freshly grated Parmesan cheese
3 × 15 ml spoons/3 tablespoons olive oil

AMERICAN
$\frac{3}{4}$ cup fresh basil leaves
3 cloves garlic, peeled
$\frac{1}{4}$ cup pine nuts
salt
$\frac{1}{4}$ cup freshly grated Parmesan cheese
3 tablespoons olive oil

Put the basil, garlic, pine nuts and salt into a mortar and pound together thoroughly. Stir in the Parmesan cheese and pound until smooth and thick. Gradually add the oil, drop by drop. This should give a creamy sauce which is just a little difficult to pour.

Add 1 × 15 ml spoon/1 tablespoon or more to vegetable soups such as minestrone, and to meat sauces served with pasta.
MAKES 3 TO 4 × 15 ml SPOONS/3 TO 4 TABLESPOONS SAUCE

Variation:
Chopped walnuts can be used instead of pine nuts.

Tarragon and Lemon Dressing

METRIC/IMPERIAL
grated rind $\frac{1}{2}$ lemon
150 ml/$\frac{1}{4}$ pint olive oil
3 × 15 ml spoons/3 tablespoons lemon juice
1 × 5 ml spoon/1 teaspoon sugar
1 × 5 ml spoon/1 teaspoon chopped fresh tarragon
salt
pepper

AMERICAN
grated rind $\frac{1}{2}$ lemon
$\frac{2}{3}$ cup olive oil
3 tablespoons lemon juice
1 teaspoon sugar
1 teaspoon chopped fresh tarragon
salt
pepper

Mix the lemon rind and oil together with a wooden spoon. Beat in the lemon juice, sugar, tarragon, and salt and pepper to taste, in that order. Serve with salads.
MAKES 250 ml/8 fl oz (1 cup)

Damson Sauce

METRIC/IMPERIAL
2 kg/4 lb damsons
450 g/1 lb onions, peeled and chopped
600 ml/1 pint vinegar
25 g/1 oz salt
1 × 15 ml spoon/1 tablespoon ground cinnamon
15 g/$\frac{1}{2}$ oz root ginger, bruised
1 × 15 ml spoon/1 tablespoon allspice berries
225 g/8 oz sugar

AMERICAN
4 lb damsons
1 lb onions, peeled and chopped
2$\frac{1}{2}$ cups vinegar
$\frac{1}{4}$ cup salt
1 tablespoon ground cinnamon
$\frac{1}{2}$ tablespoon ginger root, bruised
1 tablespoon allspice berries
1 cup sugar, firmly packed

Wash the damsons and put into a pan with the prepared onions, vinegar and salt, together with the cinnamon, ginger and allspice berries tied in muslin (cheesecloth). Simmer for about 45 minutes, stirring from time to time to break up the flesh of the damsons. Remove bag of spices, then rub the pulp through a sieve (strainer) or blend in a blender or food processor. Return to the rinsed pan, add the sugar and simmer for a further 45 minutes or until the sauce is a thick pouring consistency. Pour into heated jars and seal while hot. Allow to mature for 1 to 2 months before using, with roast or cooked meats.
MAKES ABOUT 900 ml/1$\frac{1}{2}$ PINTS/3$\frac{3}{4}$ CUPS

Variation:
Plums can be used instead of damsons in which case reduce the amount of cinnamon by half.

Basic Tomato Sauce

METRIC/IMPERIAL
2 × 15 ml spoons/2 tablespoons oil
1 small onion, peeled and very finely chopped
1 small clove garlic, crushed
1 × 397 g/14 oz can tomatoes
1 × 15 ml spoon/1 tablespoon tomato purée
1–2 × 5 ml spoons/1–2 teaspoons sugar
salt
freshly ground black pepper
1 bouquet garni

AMERICAN
2 tablespoons oil
1 small onion, peeled and very finely chopped
1 small clove garlic, crushed
1 can (16 oz) tomatoes
1 tablespoon tomato paste
1–2 teaspoons sugar
salt
freshly ground black pepper
1 bouquet garni

Heat the oil in a saucepan and sauté the onion very gently for 5 minutes until beginning to soften. Add the garlic and cook for 1 minute, then add the tomatoes and their juice, the tomato purée (paste), sugar, and salt and pepper to taste. Mash with a potato masher or wooden spoon to break up the large pieces of tomato. Bring to the boil, add the bouquet garni, cover and simmer gently for about 40 minutes. Check the seasoning, remove the bouquet garni and use the sauce as required. For a smooth-textured sauce press the contents of the pan through a sieve (strainer), or purée in a blender or food processor, and reheat.
MAKES ABOUT 300 ml/$\frac{1}{2}$ PINT (1$\frac{1}{4}$ CUPS)

Horseradish Sauce with Walnuts; Tarragon and Lemon Dressing; Pesto Sauce; Damson Sauce

Desserts

Apple and Apricot Pie

METRIC/IMPERIAL	AMERICAN
150 g/6 oz quick flaky pastry, made with 150 g/6 oz plain flour, pinch salt, 100 g/4 oz hard margarine, 6 tablespoons cold water	*6 oz quick flaky pastry, made with 1½ cups all-purpose flour, pinch salt, ½ cup hard margarine, 6 tablespoons cold water*
2 medium cooking apples, peeled, cored and sliced	*2 medium tart apples, peeled, cored and sliced*
1 × 425 g/15 oz can apricots, drained	*1 can (16 oz) apricots, drained*
25 g/1 oz granulated sugar	*2 tablespoons sugar, firmly packed*
1 × 1.25 ml spoon/¼ teaspoon ground mixed spice	*¼ teaspoon ground apple pie spice*
beaten egg to glaze	*beaten egg to glaze*

Chill the pastry (dough) in the refrigerator for 1 hour after making. Put the sliced apples into a pie dish and mix in the apricots. Combine together the sugar and mixed spice in a bowl and sprinkle them over the fruit. Roll out the pastry (dough) into an oblong shape 2.5 cm/1 inch larger than the dish. Cut a strip of pastry (dough) 5 mm/¼ inch wide off the outer edge to extend around the rim of the pie dish. Wet the rim, then place the pastry (dough) strip in position. Damp the pastry (dough) strip with water and top the pie with the remaining pastry (dough), sealing edges well together. Flute the edges with fingers or crimp with a fork. Glaze with beaten egg. Make a slit in the centre to allow the steam to escape.

Bake on a baking sheet in a preheated hot oven (220°C/425°F, Gas Mark 7) for 15 minutes. Reduce the heat to moderate (180°C/350°F, Gas Mark 4) for a further 20 minutes to cook the filling thoroughly. If necessary, cover the pie with greaseproof (waxed) paper to prevent it overbrowning. Serve with pouring cream or ice cream.

SERVES 4

Variation:
Replace the apple and apricot with canned cherries and use shortcrust pastry (basic pie dough).
Note: You can also use frozen shortcrust (basic pie dough) or puff pastry.

Banana and Ginger Pancakes (Crêpes)

METRIC/IMPERIAL	AMERICAN
100 g/4 oz plain flour	*1 cup all-purpose flour*
1 egg	*1 egg*
300 ml/½ pint milk	*1¼ cups milk*
oil or lard for frying	*oil or lard for frying*
Filling:	Filling:
6 under-ripe bananas	*6 under-ripe bananas*
lemon juice	*lemon juice*
50 g/2 oz caster sugar	*¼ cup sugar*
2 × 5 ml spoons/2 teaspoons ground ginger	*2 teaspoons ground ginger*
50 g/2 oz butter	*¼ cup butter*

To make the pancake (crêpe) batter, sift the flour into a bowl, make a well in the centre and drop in the egg. Beat with a wooden spoon and gradually add half the milk. Bring in the flour from the sides, stirring until well blended and smooth. Stir in the remaining milk. In a lightly greased 20 cm/8 inch frying pan (skillet) use the batter to make 8 thin pancakes (crêpes). Layer the pancakes (crêpes) flat on a plate with a piece of greaseproof (waxed) paper between each one.

To make the filling, peel the bananas and cut them in half lengthwise and widthwise. Dredge the bananas in lemon juice. Mix together the sugar and the ginger. Heat 25 g/1 oz (2 tablespoons) of the butter in a frying pan (skillet) and lightly fry the bananas until just beginning to brown. Remove them from the pan (skillet) with a slotted spoon and toss in the sugar and ginger. Divide the bananas equally between the pancakes (crêpes). Fold over the sides of each pancake (crêpe) and arrange in a buttered ovenproof dish. Melt the remaining butter and pour it over the pancakes (crêpes). Cover and bake in a preheated moderately hot oven (190°C/375°F, Gas Mark 5) for 20 minutes until heated through. Serve with lemon quarters and cream.

SERVES 4

Spiced Apple Pudding

METRIC/IMPERIAL	AMERICAN
50 g/2 oz butter, softened	*¼ cup butter, softened*
75 g/3 oz brown sugar	*½ cup brown sugar, firmly packed*
1 egg, beaten	*1 egg, beaten*
175 g/6 oz golden syrup	*½ cup light or dark corn syrup*
1 × 15 ml spoon/1 tablespoon finely grated orange rind	*1 tablespoon finely grated orange rind*
175 g/6 oz flour, sifted	*1½ cups flour, sifted*
1 × 2.5 ml spoon/½ teaspoon bicarbonate of soda	*½ teaspoon baking soda*
1 × 5 ml spoon/1 teaspoon each ground ginger, grated nutmeg and ground cinnamon	*1 teaspoon each ground ginger, grated nutmeg and ground cinnamon*
120 ml/4 fl oz buttermilk or milk soured with a little lemon juice	*½ cup buttermilk or milk soured with a little lemon juice*
1 apple, unpeeled and chopped	*1 apple, unpeeled and chopped*
Spicy Hard Sauce (see below, optional)	*Spicy Hard Sauce (see below, optional)*

Cream the butter and sugar until light and fluffy. Beat in the egg, golden (corn) syrup and orange rind. Sift the flour with the bicarbonate of soda (baking) and spices and add to the creamed mixture alternately with the buttermilk or soured milk. Fold in the chopped apple. Spoon into a greased 6 cup mould, cover with a double thickness of greased greaseproof (waxed) paper or aluminium foil, or a snap-on lid, and steam for 1½ hours. Unmould and serve with Spicy Hard Sauce.

SERVES 6

Spicy Hard Sauce

Cream 50 g/2 oz/¼ cup butter with 75 g/3 oz icing sugar (¾ cup confectioners sugar). Add a pinch salt, 1 × 15 ml spoon/1 tablespoon lemon juice, 1 × 5 ml spoon/1 teaspoon vanilla essence and 2 × 5 ml spoons/2 teaspoons ground mixed spice (apple pie spice). Beat until light and fluffy, then chill. Serve cold on a hot pudding.

SERVES 6

Apple and Apricot Pie

Light Fruit Pudding

METRIC/IMPERIAL

175 g/6 oz self-raising flour
pinch salt
pinch each grated nutmeg, ground cinnamon and ground ginger
100 g/4 oz butter or margarine, softened
100 g/4 oz soft brown sugar
2 eggs
1 × 5 ml spoon/1 teaspoon grated lemon rind
75 g/3 oz dried mixed fruit
3 × 15 ml spoons/3 tablespoons milk

AMERICAN

$1\frac{1}{2}$ cups self-raising flour
pinch salt
pinch each grated nutmeg, ground cinnamon and ground ginger
$\frac{1}{2}$ cup butter or margarine, softened
$\frac{2}{3}$ cup firmly packed light brown sugar
2 eggs
1 teaspoon grated lemon rind
$\frac{1}{2}$ cup dried mixed fruit
3 tablespoons milk

Sift the flour with the salt and spices. Cream the butter or margarine and brown sugar until light and fluffy, then beat in the eggs and lemon rind. (If beating by hand, the eggs should be beaten first.) Stir in the fruit, then fold in the spiced flour alternately with the milk. Spoon into a well-buttered 4 to 5 cup pudding basin (heatproof mixing bowl). Cover with a double thickness of buttered greaseproof (waxed) paper or aluminium foil, or a snap-on lid, and steam for 2 hours. Add extra boiling water when necessary. When cooked, remove the paper or lid and unmould on to a hot dish. Serve hot with custard, cream, ice cream or jam.

SERVES 4 TO 6

Ginger Soufflé

METRIC/IMPERIAL

75 g/3 oz butter
25 g/1 oz flour
250 ml/8 fl oz milk
75 g/3 oz sugar
pinch salt
4 × 5 ml spoons/4 teaspoons brandy
good pinch ground ginger
75 g/3 oz stem or crystallized ginger, drained and finely chopped
4 eggs, separated

AMERICAN

$\frac{1}{3}$ cup butter
2 tablespoons flour
1 cup milk
6 tablespoons sugar
pinch salt
4 teaspoons brandy
good pinch ground ginger
$\frac{1}{3}$ cup preserved or candied ginger, finely chopped
4 eggs, separated

In a large pan, melt the butter, add the flour and stir with a wire whisk until blended. Meanwhile, bring the milk to a boil in another pan, and add all at once to the blended roux mixture, stirring vigorously with the whisk. Bring to the boil, stirring constantly, until the sauce is thick and smooth. Add the sugar, salt, brandy and gingers. Remove from the heat and cool slightly. Beat in the egg yolks one at a time. Cool. Whisk the egg whites with a pinch of salt until they stand in soft peaks and fold into the mixture. Place in a 2 litre/$3\frac{1}{2}$ pint ($4\frac{1}{2}$ pint) soufflé dish and bake in preheated moderately hot oven (190°C/375°F, Gas Mark 5) for 35 to 45 minutes. Serve immediately.

SERVES 6

Catalan Creme Caramel

Fresh Fruit Salad with Borage

METRIC/IMPERIAL

1 small pineapple, skin and core removed and flesh diced
3 oranges, cut up into segments
2 apples, peeled, cored and sliced
2 pears, peeled, cored and sliced
juice 1 lemon
25 g/1 oz black or green grapes, halved and seeded
1 × 227 g/8 oz can lychees in syrup
1 sprig mint, chopped
3 × 15 ml spoons/3 tablespoons borage, chopped

AMERICAN

1 small pineapple, skin and core removed, and flesh diced
3 oranges, cut up into segments
2 apples, peeled, cored and sliced
2 pears, peeled, cored and sliced
juice 1 lemon
$\frac{1}{4}$ cup black or green grapes, halved and seeded
1 can ($8\frac{1}{4}$ oz) lychees in syrup
1 sprig mint, chopped
3 tablespoons borage, chopped

Put the pineapple, oranges, apples and pears into a large mixing bowl, stir in the lemon juice and mix well. Stir in the grapes and lychees and their syrup. Sprinkle over the chopped mint and borage and mix well. Cover and refrigerate for 1 hour. Serve with crisp shortbread and whipped cream.

SERVES 4 TO 6

Gingered Pear and Yogurt Mousse

METRIC/IMPERIAL	AMERICAN
1 kg/2 lb pears, peeled, cored and chopped	*2 lb pears, peeled, cored and chopped*
finely grated rind and juice of 1 lemon	*finely grated rind and juice of 1 lemon*
1 × 1.25 ml spoon/¼ teaspoon ground ginger	*¼ teaspoon ground ginger*
3–4 pieces stem ginger in syrup	*3–4 pieces preserved ginger in syrup*
2 eggs, separated	*2 eggs, separated*
300 ml/½ pint natural yogurt	*1¼ cups natural yogurt*
15 g/½ oz gelatine	*2 envelopes unflavored gelatine*
2 tablespoons water	*2 tablespoons water*

Put the pears in a pan with the lemon rind and juice, ginger and 2 tablespoons syrup from the stem (preserved) ginger. Cover and cook gently for 10 to 15 minutes until the pears are tender, stirring occasionally. Take out the stem (preserved) ginger; chop one of the pieces, slice the remainder and set aside. Put the pears and juice, egg yolks and yogurt in a blender or food processor and blend to a smooth puree. Alternatively, rub the pears and juice through a sieve (strainer), then beat in the egg yolks and yogurt.

Sprinkle the gelatine over the water in a small cup. Stand the cup in a pan of hot water and stir until the gelatine has dissolved. Stir into the pear purée, with the chopped ginger. Leave in a cool place until thick and just beginning to set. Whisk the egg whites until stiff, then fold into the mixture. Spoon into 6 individual glasses or dishes and chill in the refrigerator until set. Decorate with slices of stem (preserved) ginger. Serve chilled.

SERVES 6

Catalan Creme Caramel

METRIC/IMPERIAL	AMERICAN
600 ml/1 pint milk	*2½ cups milk*
1 stick cinnamon	*1 stick cinnamon*
grated rind 1 lemon	*grated rind 1 lemon*
6 egg yolks	*6 egg yolks*
3 tablespoons cornflour	*3 tablespoons cornstarch*
100 g/4 oz sugar	*½ cup sugar*

Heat three-quarters of the milk in a saucepan with the cinnamon stick and lemon rind. Bring to the boil and simmer gently for 5 minutes. Add half of the remaining milk to the egg yolks and whisk thoroughly. Blend the cornflour (cornstarch) with the remaining milk. Strain the hot milk into a clean pan. Add all but 2 × 15 ml spoons/2 tablespoons of the sugar, the egg yolk mixture and blended cornflour (cornstarch). Place over a very low heat and stir constantly until the custard thickens. Pour into shallow heatproof serving dishes and allow to cool. When the custard has set, sprinkle the remaining sugar evenly over the surface and place under a hot grill (broiler) until the sugar turns golden brown. Chill before serving.

SERVES 4

Cinnamon Compote of Summer Fruits

METRIC/IMPERIAL	AMERICAN
150 ml/¼ pint water	*⅔ cup water*
75 g/3 oz granulated sugar	*6 tablespoons sugar*
1 stick cinnamon	*1 stick cinnamon*
thinly pared rind 1 orange	*thinly pared rind 1 orange*
150 ml/¼ pint red wine	*⅔ cup red wine*
100 g/4 oz fresh raspberries	*1 cup fresh raspberries*
225 g/8 oz fresh strawberries	*1⅔ cups fresh strawberries*
100 g/4 oz fresh redcurrants	*1 cup fresh red currants*
100 g/4 oz fresh blackcurrants	*1 cup fresh black currants*

Put the water, sugar, cinnamon stick and orange rind into a pan and gradually bring to the boil, stirring to dissolve the sugar. Stir in the wine, boil for 2 minutes, remove from the heat and leave to cool. Prepare the soft fruits: hull the raspberries and strawberries and wipe over if necessary; string the currants and put the fruit into a serving dish. Spoon over the cooled syrup. Cover and refrigerate for 1 hour. Serve chilled with whipped cream.

SERVES 4 TO 6

Minted Apple Snow

METRIC/IMPERIAL
1 kg/2 lb cooking apples, peeled, cored and sliced
finely grated rind and juice 1 orange
3 × 15 ml spoons/3 tablespoons honey
4 large sprigs mint
2 large egg whites

AMERICAN
2 lb tart apples, peeled, cored and sliced
finely grated rind and juice 1 orange
3 tablespoons honey
4 large sprigs mint
2 large egg whites

Put the apples in a pan, then add the orange rind and juice and the honey. Add the mint, reserving the top leaves for decoration. Cover and cook gently for about 15 minutes until the apples are cooked to a pulp, stirring occasionally. Discard the mint, then beat the pulp vigorously with a wooden spoon until smooth. Alternatively, rub through a sieve (strainer) or purée in a blender or food processor. Leave to cool. Whisk the egg whites until stiff, then fold into the apple purée (apple sauce). Spoon into a serving bowl or individual dishes or glasses. Decorate with the reserved mint leaves. Serve chilled.
SERVES 4

Mint Ice Cream

METRIC/IMPERIAL
5 egg yolks
3 × 15 ml spoons/3 tablespoons vanilla sugar
pinch salt
300 ml/½ pint double cream
1 vanilla pod
3 × 15 ml spoons/3 tablespoons chopped fresh spearmint
sprigs mint to decorate
water biscuits to serve

AMERICAN
5 egg yolks
3 tablespoons vanilla sugar
pinch salt
1½ cups heavy cream
1 vanilla bean
3 tablespoons chopped fresh spearmint
sprigs mint to decorate
water biscuits to serve

Turn the refrigerator to its lowest setting. Combine the egg yolks and vanilla sugar together, add the salt and whisk until light and fluffy. Put the cream and vanilla pod (bean) into a pan, bring to the boil and cook for 1 minute. Strain the flavoured cream into the egg mixture and whisk well. Pour the mixture into a basin over a pan of hot water (double boiler) and stir constantly until the custard thickens, taking care that the mixture does not boil or it will curdle. Strain the custard through a fine sieve (strainer) and allow to cool.

Stir in the spearmint. Pour the mint custard into a freezing tray and freeze until half frozen, stirring the mixture occasionally. Remove from the freezer and mix thoroughly, and then return to the freezer and leave until set. Transfer the mint ice cream to the refrigerator 1 hour before serving. Garnish with sprigs of fresh mint and serve with water biscuits.
SERVES 4 TO 6

Fruit Fondue

METRIC/IMPERIAL
selection of fresh fruits, such as pineapple, apples, bananas, melon, grapes, cherries, strawberries or oranges
Sauce:
250 ml/8 fl oz soured cream
25 g/1 oz desiccated coconut
2 × 15 ml spoons/2 tablespoons chopped walnuts
2 × 15 ml spoons/2 tablespoons sieved apricot jam
2 × 5 ml spoons/2 teaspoons finely chopped stem ginger

AMERICAN
selection of fresh fruits, such as pineapple, apples, bananas, melon, grapes, cherries, strawberries or oranges
Sauce:
1 cup sour cream
¼ cup shredded coconut
2 tablespoons chopped walnuts
2 tablespoons strained apricot jam
2 teaspoons finely chopped stem ginger

Combine all the ingredients for the sauce and divide among 4 small bowls. Arrange a selection of sliced fruits on 4 individual plates for dipping. Place a bowl of sauce in the centre of each plate of fruit. Chill before serving.
SERVES 4

Spiced Stuffed Peaches

METRIC/IMPERIAL
4 large peaches
juice 2 oranges
2 × 15 ml spoons/2 tablespoons redcurrant jelly
1 stick cinnamon
2 whole cloves
1 × 2.5 ml spoon/½ teaspoon allspice berries
2–3 tablespoons brandy (optional)
Filling:
1 egg, lightly beaten
50 g/2 oz ground almonds
1 × 15 ml spoon/1 tablespoon finely chopped stem ginger
1 × 15 ml spoon/1 tablespoon soft brown sugar

AMERICAN
4 large peaches
juice 2 oranges
2 tablespoons red currant jelly
1 stick cinnamon
2 whole cloves
½ teaspoon allspice berries
2–3 tablespoons brandy (optional)
Filling:
1 egg, lightly beaten
½ cup ground almonds
1 tablespoon finely chopped preserved ginger
1 tablespoon light brown sugar

Cut the peaches in half. Remove the stones (seeds). Scoop out and reserve some of the flesh from the centre of each peach half to allow room for the filling. To make the filling, put the egg in a bowl with the almonds, ginger, sugar and reserved peach flesh. Mix well, then spoon into the peach halves. Place the peaches in a baking dish. Put the orange juice, redcurrant jelly and spices in a small pan. Heat gently until the jelly has dissolved, then bring to the boil. Pour over the peaches. Bake in a preheated moderate oven (180°C/350°F, Gas Mark 4) for about 20 minutes until the peaches are tender when pierced with a skewer. If liked, warm the brandy, pour over the peaches and ignite. Serve hot or cold.
SERVES 4

Blackberry and Orange Stuffed Apples; Spiced Stuffed Peaches

Blackberry and Orange Stuffed Apples

METRIC/IMPERIAL
4 large cooking apples
225 g/8 oz blackberries
finely grated rind and juice 1 large orange
4 × 15 ml spoons/4 tablespoons soft brown sugar
1 × 15 ml spoon/1 tablespoon chopped fresh mint

AMERICAN
4 large tart apples
2 cups blackberries
finely grated rind and juice 1 large orange
⅔ cup firmly packed light brown sugar
1 tablespoon chopped fresh mint

Remove the cores from the apples, making a large hole for the stuffing. Make a shallow cut through the skin around the centre of each apple to prevent the skins bursting. To make the stuffing, mix the blackberries with the orange rind, sugar and mint. Place the apples in a baking dish and divide the stuffing equally between the apples, pressing it well down the centres. Spoon any remaining stuffing around the apples, then spoon over the orange juice. Bake in a preheated moderate oven (180°C/350°F, Gas Mark 4) for 45 minutes or until the apples are tender. Serve hot.
SERVES 4

Cakes & Biscuits

Pumpkin Spice Cake

METRIC/IMPERIAL

100 g/4 oz butter, softened
275 g/10 oz caster sugar
2 eggs
250 g/9 oz self-raising flour
1 × 2.5 ml spoon/½ teaspoon salt
1 × 5 ml spoon/1 teaspoon ground cinnamon
1 × 5 ml spoon/1 teaspoon ground ginger
1 × 5 ml spoon/1 teaspoon grated nutmeg
1 × 1.25 ml spoon/¼ teaspoon ground cloves
175 ml/6 fl oz milk
250 g/8 oz cooked, drained and mashed pumpkin
½ × 5 ml spoon/½ teaspoon bicarbonate of soda
50 g/2 oz chopped walnuts

AMERICAN

½ cup butter, softened
1¼ cups sugar
2 eggs
2¼ cups self-rising flour
½ teaspoon salt
1 teaspoon ground cinnamon
1 teaspoon ground ginger
1 teaspoon grated nutmeg
¼ teaspoon ground cloves
¾ cup milk
1 cup cooked, drained and mashed pumpkin
½ teaspoon baking soda
½ cup chopped walnuts

Grease a rectangular cake tin (pan) about 33 × 23 cm/13 × 9 inches and line the base with greased greaseproof (waxed) paper. Cream the butter and sugar together until light and fluffy, then beat in the eggs one at a time. Sift together the flour, salt and spices. In another bowl, combine the milk with the pumpkin and bicarbonate of soda (baking soda). Add the flour and pumpkin mixtures alternately to the creamed mixture, beginning and ending with flour. Stir in the nuts. Turn into the prepared tin (pan) and bake in a preheated moderate oven (180°C/350°F, Gas Mark 4) for 50 to 55 minutes, or until cooked when tested with a skewer. Cool in the tin (pan) for a few minutes, then invert on to a wire rack to finish cooling.

Note: Pumpkin Spice Cake will keep moist in an airtight container for about 1 week.

Crunch-topped Spice Cake

METRIC/IMPERIAL

225 g/8 oz self-raising flour
1 × 5 ml spoon/1 teaspoon ground cinnamon
1 × 5 ml spoon/1 teaspoon ground mixed spice
½ × 5 ml spoon/½ teaspoon ground coriander
175 g/6 oz butter or hard margarine
175 g/6 oz caster sugar
3 eggs
100 g/4 oz glacé cherries, quartered
50 g/2 oz mixed peel
50 g/2 oz cornflakes, crushed
2 × 15 ml spoons/2 tablespoons golden syrup, slightly warmed

AMERICAN

2 cups self-rising flour
1 teaspoon ground cinnamon
1 teaspoon ground allspice
½ teaspoon ground coriander
¾ cup butter or hard margarine
¾ cup sugar
3 eggs
½ cup glacé cherries quartered
⅓ cup candied peel
2 cups cornflakes, crushed
2 tablespoons corn syrup, slightly warmed

Grease and flour a 23 cm/9 inch springform cake tin (pan) fitted with a tubular base, or a 20 cm/8 inch round cake tin (pan). Line the sides with a greased piece of greaseproof (waxed) paper. Sift the flour and spices together into a mixing bowl. Using a wooden spoon, cream the fat and sugar together in a mixing bowl until light and fluffy. Beat in the eggs one at a time, then stir in the sifted flour and spices until completely mixed. Stir in the cherries and the mixed (candied) peel. Spoon the mixture into the prepared tin (pan) and spread evenly. Stir the cornflakes into the syrup and carefully spread the mixture over the cake.

Bake in a preheated moderate oven (180°C/350°F, Gas Mark 4) for 30 minutes, then reduce the oven temperature to 160°C/325°F, Gas Mark 3 for a further 30 minutes for the springform tin (pan), or 40 minutes for the round cake tin (pan), until it is well risen and firm to the touch. Allow the cake to cool in the tin (pan) for a few minutes, then remove the sides of the tin (pan) and invert the cake on to a wire rack to remove the base. Turn the cake over and allow it to cool completely.

Rich Fruit Cake

Rich Fruit Cake

METRIC/IMPERIAL
225 g/8 oz raisins
225 g/8 oz currants
225 g/8 oz sultanas
225 g/8 oz plain flour
1 × 5 ml spoon/1 teaspoon ground mace
1 × 5 ml spoon/1 teaspoon ground mixed spice
225 g/8 oz butter
200 g/7 oz dark brown sugar
1 × 15 ml spoon/1 tablespoon black treacle
4 eggs
100 g/4 oz glacé cherries, quartered
100 g/4 oz mixed peel
finely grated rind 1 lemon
25 g/1 oz angelica, chopped
During storage:
3–4 × 15 ml spoons/3 to 4 tablespoons brandy

AMERICAN
1¼ cups raisins
1¼ cups currants
1¼ cups golden raisins
2 cups all-purpose flour
1 teaspoon ground mace
1 teaspoon ground allspice
1 cup butter
1 cup plus 1 tablespoon firmly packed dark brown sugar
1 tablespoon molasses
4 eggs
½ cup candied cherries, quartered
¼ cup candied peel
finely grated rind 1 lemon
3 tablespoons angelica, chopped
During storage:
3–4 tablespoons brandy

Grease and line a 20 cm/8 inch round, or 18 cm/7 inch square, cake tin (pan) with greaseproof (waxed) paper. Place all the prepared fruit in a large bowl. Sift the flour and spices together on to a sheet of greaseproof (waxed) paper. Using a wooden spoon, cream the butter, sugar and treacle (molasses) together until light and fluffy. Beat in the eggs, one at a time, then stir in the flour and spices, using a metal spoon. Stir in the fruit, cherries, peel, lemon rind and angelica. Spoon the mixture into the prepared cake tin (pan). Wrap a band of brown paper or newspaper around the outside of the tin (pan).

Bake, just below the centre of a preheated cool oven (150°C/300°F, Gas Mark 2) for the first 2 hours. Reduce the oven temperature to 140°C/275°F, Gas Mark 1, for a further 1½ to 2 hours. Test to see if the cake is cooked through by inserting a skewer or fine knitting needle into the centre of the cake. If the skewer comes out clean, the cake is cooked. Otherwise cook the cake for a further 20 to 30 minutes. Allow the cake to cool for 15 minutes in the tin (pan). Invert on to a wire rack to cool.

When completely cold, wrap the cake in aluminium foil. The cake will store for up to 3 months, wrapped in this way, in a cool, dry place. During storage, prick the surface of the cake with a fine skewer and pour the brandy over the cake.

Note: To royal ice the cake, it is necessary to almond paste it first; 750 g/1¾ lb almond paste is sufficient for this size cake, and 1 kg/2 lb royal icing will be needed.

Dorset Apple Cake

METRIC/IMPERIAL
225 g/8 oz self-raising flour
½ × 5 ml spoon/½ teaspoon ground cloves
100 g/4 oz butter, softened
100 g/4 oz soft brown sugar
225 g/8 oz eating apples, peeled and grated
2 eggs, beaten
2 × 15 ml spoons/2 tablespoons soft brown sugar
pinch freshly grated nutmeg
pinch ground cinnamon
pinch ground cloves

AMERICAN
2 cups self-rising flour
½ teaspoon ground cloves
½ cup butter, softened
⅔ cup firmly packed light brown sugar
½ lb eating apples, peeled and grated
2 eggs, beaten
2 tablespoons firmly packed light brown sugar
pinch freshly grated nutmeg
pinch ground cinnamon
pinch ground cloves

Grease and line a 23 cm/9 inch round cake tin (pan). Sift the flour and ½ × 5 ml spoon/½ teaspoon ground cloves into a mixing bowl and rub in (cut in) the butter until the mixture resembles fine breadcrumbs. Stir in the 100 g/4 oz/⅔ cup brown sugar, apples and eggs. Stir the mixture into a fairly stiff dough (batter) and spread it over the base of the prepared tin (pan). Mix the remaining sugar and spices together and sprinkle over the top of the cake. Bake in a preheated moderately hot oven (190°C/375°F, Gas Mark 5) for 30 minutes, then reduce the temperature to moderate (180°C/350°F, Gas Mark 4). Cover the top of the cake with greaseproof (waxed) paper and continue cooking for a further 25 to 30 minutes, until the cake is well risen and golden brown. Cool for 10 minutes in the tin (pan), then transfer to a wire rack. Store in an airtight tin.

Sticky Orange and Almond Gingerbread

Beer and Date Cake

METRIC/IMPERIAL	AMERICAN
225 g/8 oz butter	*1 cup butter*
275 g/10 oz brown sugar	*2 cups firmly packed brown sugar*
2 eggs	*2 eggs*
100 g/4 oz chopped walnuts	*1 cup chopped walnuts*
150 g/5 oz chopped dates	*1 cup chopped dates*
350 g/12 oz plain flour	*3 cups all-purpose flour*
1 × 2.5 ml spoon/½ teaspoon salt	*½ teaspoon salt*
2 × 5 ml spoons/2 teaspoons bicarbonate of soda	*2 teaspoons baking soda*
1 × 5 ml spoon/1 teaspoon ground cinnamon	*1 teaspoon ground cinnamon*
1 × 2.5 ml spoon/½ teaspoon mixed spice	*½ teaspoon apple pie spice*
1 × 2.5 ml spoon/½ teaspoon ground cloves	*½ teaspoon ground cloves*
450 ml/¾ pint beer	*2 cups beer*

Cream the butter and sugar together in a bowl until light and fluffy. Add the eggs, one at a time, beating well after each addition. Stir in the nuts and dates. Sift the flour, salt, soda and spices together. Fold in the flour alternately with the beer, beginning and ending with the flour. Spoon into a greased 2.25 litre/4 pint (5 pint) bundt tin. Bake in a preheated moderate oven (180°C/350°F, Gas Mark 4) for 1 to 1¼ hours or until a fine skewer inserted in the centre comes out clean. Invert cake on to a wire rack and cool.

Sticky Orange and Almond Gingerbread

METRIC/IMPERIAL	AMERICAN
275 g/10 oz plain flour	*2½ cups all-purpose flour*
1 × 5 ml spoon/1 teaspoon bicarbonate of soda	*1 teaspoon baking soda*
2 × 5 ml spoons/2 teaspoons ground ginger	*2 teaspoons ground ginger*
1 × 5 ml spoon/1 teaspoon ground mixed spice	*1 teaspoon ground allspice*
175 g/6 oz margarine	*¾ cup margarine*
400 g/14 oz golden syrup	*1¼ cups corn syrup*
50 g/2 oz caster sugar	*¼ cup sugar*
2 eggs	*2 eggs*
120 ml/4 fl oz milk	*½ cup milk*
2 × 15 ml spoons/2 tablespoons fresh orange juice	*2 tablespoons fresh orange juice*
50 g/2 oz nibbed almonds	*½ cup nibbed almonds*
finely grated rind 1 orange	*finely grated rind 1 orange*
2 to 3 × 15 ml spoons/2 to 3 tablespoons golden syrup to glaze	*2 to 3 tablespoons corn syrup to glaze*
strips orange peel, finely cut, to decorate	*strips orange peel, finely cut, to decorate*

Grease well and flour a 23 cm/9 inch round cake tin (pan). Sift together the flour, soda, ginger and spice into a large bowl. Warm the margarine, syrup and sugar in a saucepan over a low heat. Beat together the eggs and milk. Make a well in the centre of the dry ingredients and add the milk mixture and orange juice. Gradually incorporate the flour from the sides to the centre. Pour in the syrup mixture a little at a time, beating well. Stir in the almonds and orange rind.

Pour the batter into the prepared tin (pan), and bake in the centre of a preheated moderate oven (180°C/350°F, Gas Mark 4) for about 1 hour. Leave to cool for a few minutes in the tin (pan), then invert on to a wire rack. Heat the syrup in a saucepan and brush it over the surface of the cake. Sprinkle with the strips of orange peel.

Grandma's Chocolate Bars

METRIC/IMPERIAL	AMERICAN
425 g/15 oz brown sugar	*2½ cups firmly packed brown sugar*
6 eggs	*6 eggs*
100 g/4 oz dark chocolate, grated	*4 squares dark chocolate, grated*
350 g/12 oz plain flour	*3 cups all-purpose flour*
1 × 15 ml spoon/1 tablespoon ground cinnamon	*1 tablespoon ground cinnamon*
1.5 × 5 ml spoons/1½ teaspoons ground cloves	*1½ teaspoon ground cloves*
1 × 5 ml spoon/1 teaspoon ground allspice	*1 teaspoon ground allspice*
1 × 5 ml spoon/1 teaspoon bicarbonate of soda	*1 teaspoon baking soda*
1 × 5 ml spoon/1 teaspoon salt	*1 teaspoon salt*
175 g/6 oz honey	*½ cup honey*
300 g/10 oz mixed peel	*2 cups candied peel*
50 g/2 oz blanched almonds, chopped	*½ cup chopped almonds*
Chocolate Icing (see below)	*Chocolate Frosting* (see below)

Grease two rectangular cake tins (pans) 23 × 33 cm/9 × 13 inches. Sift the sugar to remove any lumps. Beat the eggs until light, then gradually beat in the sugar and stir in the chocolate. Sift together the flour, spices, soda and salt. Add to the egg mixture alternately with the honey, beginning and ending with flour. Chop the peel and stir in with almonds. Spread the batter evenly in the two tins (pans), and bake for 25 minutes in a preheated moderate oven (180°C/350°F, Gas Mark 4) or until a skewer inserted in the mixture comes out clean. Cool in the tins (pans), then ice and cut into bars.

MAKES ABOUT 100 SMALL BARS

Chocolate Icing (Frosting)

METRIC/IMPERIAL	AMERICAN
75 g/3 oz dark chocolate	*3 squares dark chocolate*
25 g/1 oz butter	*2 tablespoons butter*
4 × 15 ml spoons/4 tablespoons hot black coffee	*¼ cup hot black coffee*
1 egg, lightly beaten	*1 egg, lightly beaten*
pinch salt	*pinch salt*
1 × 5 ml spoon/1 teaspoon vanilla essence	*1 teaspoon vanilla*
325 g/11 oz icing sugar, sifted	*2½ cups confectioners' sugar, sifted*

Place the chocolate and butter in a basin over a pan of hot water (double boiler) and stir until melted. Remove from the heat and blend in the coffee, egg, salt and vanilla. When cool, stir in the icing (confectioner's) sugar until the mixture is a good spreading consistency.

Light Peppernuts

METRIC/IMPERIAL

100 g/4 oz butter
100 g/4 oz caster sugar
2 eggs, well beaten
100 g/4 oz plain flour
1 × 1.25 ml spoon/$\frac{1}{4}$ teaspoon salt
1 × 1.25 ml spoon/$\frac{1}{4}$ teaspoon bicarbonate of soda
1 × 2.5 ml spoon/$\frac{1}{2}$ teaspoon each ground black pepper, grated nutmeg, ground cloves and ground allspice
1 × 5 ml spoon/1 teaspoon ground cinnamon
good pinch crushed anise seeds
good pinch ground cardamom
25 g/1 oz ground almonds
275 g/9 oz mixed peel, chopped

AMERICAN

$\frac{1}{2}$ cup butter
$\frac{1}{2}$ cup sugar
2 eggs, well beaten
1 cup all-purpose flour
$\frac{1}{4}$ teaspoon salt
$\frac{1}{4}$ teaspoon baking soda
$\frac{1}{2}$ teaspoon each ground black pepper, grated nutmeg, ground cloves and ground allspice
1 teaspoon ground cinnamon
good pinch crushed anise seeds
good pinch ground cardamon
$\frac{1}{4}$ cup ground almonds
$1\frac{3}{4}$ cups chopped candied peel

Cream the butter and sugar well together in a mixing bowl, then gradually beat in the eggs. Sift the flour with salt, bicarbonate and spices and stir into the creamed mixture. Add the almonds and peel and mix well. Drop the dough by teaspoonfuls on to well-greased baking trays, leaving about 5 cm/2 inches between the biscuits to allow for spreading. Bake in a preheated moderate oven (180°C/350°F, Gas Mark 4) for 10 to 12 minutes, until brown on top and crisp at the edges. Allow to cool a little on the trays, then remove to wire racks.
MAKES ABOUT 35

Spiced Honey Cake

METRIC/IMPERIAL

225 g/8 oz plain flour
1 × 5 ml spoon/1 teaspoon ground cinnamon
1 × 2.5 ml spoon/$\frac{1}{2}$ teaspoon grated nutmeg
1 × 2.5 ml spoon/$\frac{1}{2}$ teaspoon cream of tartar
1 × 2.5 ml spoon/$\frac{1}{2}$ teaspoon bicarbonate of soda
1 × 5 ml spoon/1 teaspoon ground cardamom
pinch salt
175 g/6 oz butter
25 g/1 oz brown sugar
4 × 5 ml spoons/4 teaspoons sugar
3 small eggs
350 g/12 oz honey
120 ml/4 fl oz soured cream
almonds to decorate

AMERICAN

2 cups all-purpose flour
1 teaspoon ground cinnamon
$\frac{1}{2}$ teaspoon grated nutmeg
$\frac{1}{2}$ teaspoon cream of tartar
$\frac{1}{2}$ teaspoon baking soda
1 teaspoon ground cardamom
pinch salt
$\frac{3}{4}$ cup butter
$2\frac{1}{2}$ tablespoons brown sugar
4 teaspoons sugar
3 small eggs
1 cup honey
$\frac{1}{2}$ cup sour cream
almonds to decorate

Line a 23 cm/9 inch square deep cake tin (pan) with greased greaseproof (waxed) paper. Sift the flour with the cinnamon, nutmeg, cream of tartar, soda, ground cardamom and salt. Melt butter and stir in the sugars. In a large bowl beat the eggs until they are very fluffy, add the honey and soured cream gradually. Add the butter mixture, stirring briskly. Gradually stir in the sifted dry ingredients. Pour batter into prepared tin (pan) and bake in a preheated moderate oven (180°C/350°F, Gas Mark 4) for 1 hour or until cake is cooked when tested with a skewer.

After 20 minutes of baking, take cake out and decorate with almonds, then continue baking for remaining time. Invert cake on to a wire rack to cool, then put in an airtight container to mature for at least 2 days before cutting. This cake keeps for several weeks.

Chocolate and Cinnamon Gâteau

METRIC/IMPERIAL

150 g/5 oz plain cooking chocolate
100 g/4 oz butter, softened
150 g/5 oz soft brown sugar
3 large eggs
100 g/4 oz ground almonds
grated rind 1 large orange
1.5 × 5 ml spoons/$1\frac{1}{2}$ teaspoons ground cinnamon
4 × 15 ml spoons/4 tablespoons fine dried breadcrumbs
Icing:
175 g/6 oz unsweetened or plain cooking chocolate
120 ml/4 fl oz double cream
50 g/2 oz butter
450 g/1 lb icing sugar, sifted
1 × 5 ml spoon/1 teaspoon ground cinnamon
walnut halves to decorate

AMERICAN

5 squares semi-sweet cooking chocolate
$\frac{1}{2}$ cup butter, softened
scant 1 cup light brown sugar
3 large eggs
1 cup ground almonds
grated rind 1 large orange
$1\frac{1}{2}$ teaspoons ground cinnamon
4 tablespoons fine dried bread crumbs
Frosting:
6 squares unsweetened or semi-sweet cooking chocolate
$\frac{1}{2}$ cup heavy cream
$\frac{1}{4}$ cup butter
1 lb confectioners' sugar, sifted
1 teaspoon ground cinnamon
walnut halves to decorate

Grease and line a 20 cm/8 inch round cake tin (pan). Melt the first lot of chocolate in a basin over a pan of hot water (double boiler). Cream the butter and sugar until very light and fluffy. Gradually beat in the eggs until thoroughly mixed (do not worry if the mixture curdles at this stage). Stir in the melted chocolate, ground almonds, orange rind, cinnamon and breadcrumbs. Spoon the mixture into the prepared tin (pan) and bake in a preheated moderately hot oven (190°C/375°F, Gas Mark 5) for 25 to 30 minutes until well risen and golden brown. Cool in the tin (pan) for 30 minutes, then invert the cake on to a wire rack until cold. Store in an airtight tin overnight.

To make the icing (frosting): put the chocolate, cream and butter in a basin over a pan of hot water (double boiler) and stir until dissolved. Remove from the heat and gradually beat in the icing (confectioners') sugar and cinnamon. Cut the cake into 2 or 3 layers (the cake should be moist in the centre). Cool the icing (frosting) for 5 minutes, then spread over the cake slices. Sandwich the slices together and spread the remaining icing (frosting) over the top and sides. Decorate with walnut halves.

Chocolate and Cinnamon Gâteau; Spiced Honey Cake

Breads

Hot Cross Buns

METRIC/IMPERIAL

450 g/1 lb strong flour
25 g/1 oz fresh yeast or 1 × 15 ml spoon/1 tablespoon dried yeast
1 × 5 ml spoon/1 teaspoon caster sugar
300 ml/½ pint milk
1 × 2.5 ml spoon/½ teaspoon ground cinnamon
pinch each grated nutmeg, ground ginger and ground cloves
1 × 5 ml spoon/1 teaspoon salt
50 g/2 oz caster sugar
50 g/2 oz butter, melted
1 egg, beaten
100 g/4 oz currants
25 g/1 oz mixed peel, chopped
To finish:
50 g/2 oz shortcrust pastry
25 g/1 oz caster sugar
3 × 15 ml spoons/3 tablespoons water

AMERICAN

4 cups strong flour
½ cake compressed yeast or 1 tablespoon active dried yeast
1 teaspoon caster sugar
1¼ cups milk
½ teaspoon ground cinnamon
pinch each grated nutmeg, ground ginger and ground cloves
1 teaspoon salt
¼ cup sugar
¼ cup butter, melted
1 egg, beaten
⅔ cup currants
3 tablespoons chopped candied peel
To finish:
2 oz basic pie dough
2 tablespoons sugar
3 tablespoons water

Grease a baking sheet. Sift 100 g/4 oz (1 cup) of the flour into a large mixing bowl and add the yeast and 1 × 5 ml spoon/1 teaspoon sugar. Warm the milk to bloodheat, add the milk to the flour and mix well. Leave in a warm place for 20 minutes if using fresh yeast and 30 minutes for dried yeast, until it becomes frothy. Sift the remaining flour, spices and salt together into a bowl and stir in the remaining sugar. Pour the butter and egg into the batter and stir well, then add the spiced flour, currants and mixed peel and combine well together.

Turn the soft dough on to a floured board and knead until smooth. Place the dough in a lightly greased plastic bag or a greased bowl, cover with a damp cloth, and leave to rise at room temperature until it has doubled in size. Put the risen dough on to the board and knead for a further 2 minutes. Shape the dough into a long roll and cut into 12 pieces. Shape the dough into buns, using the palm of the hand. Put the buns on the baking sheet and cover with oiled cling film (plastic wrap). Leave the buns to rise in a warm place until doubled in size. Roll out the pastry into a long strip and cut into 5 mm/¼ inch strips. Top each bun with the pastry strips in the shape of a cross, securing them with water. Alternatively, make slashes with a sharp knife to make a cross.

Bake just above the centre of a moderately hot oven (190°C/375°F, Gas Mark 5) for 20 to 25 minutes. Dissolve the sugar in the water and use to glaze the buns when they are removed from the oven and are still hot. Allow them to cool on a wire rack.

MAKES 12

Fruit Bread

METRIC/IMPERIAL

15 g/½ oz fresh yeast or 2 × 5 ml spoons/2 teaspoons dried yeast
250 ml/8 fl oz tepid water
25 g/1 oz caster sugar
450 g/1 lb strong flour
1 × 5 ml spoon/1 teaspoon salt
good pinch each grated nutmeg, ground ginger and ground coriander
1 × 5 ml spoon/1 teaspoon ground cinnamon
350 g/12 oz mixed dried fruit
grated rind 1 lemon
1 egg, beaten
2 × 15 ml spoons/2 tablespoons lemon juice
2 × 5 ml spoons/2 teaspoons sugar
2 × 15 ml spoons/2 tablespoons water

AMERICAN

½ compressed yeast or 2 teaspoons active dry yeast
1 cup tepid water
2 tablespoons sugar
4 cups strong flour
1 teaspoon salt
good pinch each grated nutmeg, ground ginger and ground coriander
1 teaspoon ground cinnamon
2¼ cups mixed dried fruit
grated rind 1 lemon
1 egg, beaten
2 tablespoons lemon juice
2 teaspoons sugar
2 tablespoons water

Grease a 1 kg/2 lb loaf tin (9 × 5 inch loaf pan) or two 450 g/1 lb loaf tins (7 × 3 inch loaf pans). Blend the fresh yeast with a little of the water then stir in the remaining water. Reconstitute the dried yeast by putting a little of the measured water and a pinch of sugar in a small bowl; sprinkle in the yeast granules. Stir, then leave in a warm place for 15 minutes until a frothy head appears. Stir in the remaining water. Sift together the flour, salt, and spices in a large warm mixing bowl. Stir in the remaining sugar, dried fruit and lemon rind. Pour the yeast mixture, beaten egg, and lemon juice into the dry ingredients and mix well with a wooden spoon.

Knead the dough on a lightly floured board for 10 minutes until firm and elastic. Place the dough in a greased polythene bag or a greased bowl, cover with a damp cloth, and leave to rise in a warm place until doubled in size, about 1½ hours at room temperature or 40 minutes in a warm kitchen. Turn the dough on to a floured board and knead for 2 minutes, then shape to fit into the loaf tin(s) (pans). Leave the dough to rise, covered with oiled cling film (plastic wrap), until doubled its size. Dissolve the sugar in the water and brush the surface of the loaf, then bake in the centre of a preheated moderately hot oven (200°C/400°F, Gas Mark 6) for 45 minutes for the large loaf, or 30 to 35 minutes for the smaller loaves. Remove from the tins (pans) and cool on a wire rack.

MAKES 1 OR 2 LOAVES

Fruit Bread

Easter Dove Bread

METRIC/IMPERIAL	AMERICAN
Dough:	Dough:
225 g/8 oz strong plain flour	*2 cups bread flour*
pinch salt	*pinch salt*
125 ml/4 fl oz milk	*½ cup milk*
50 g/2 oz butter	*¼ cup butter*
15 g/½ oz fresh yeast	*½ oz compressed yeast*
50 g/2 oz caster sugar	*¼ cup sugar*
1 egg, beaten	*1 egg, beaten*
8 cloves to decorate	*8 cloves to decorate*
1 egg, lightly beaten, to glaze	*1 egg, lightly beaten, to glaze*

Sift the flour with the salt into a large bowl. Heat the milk to lukewarm, then add the butter and allow to melt. Add the milk and butter mixture to the yeast, stirring until dissolved. Mix in the sugar and egg.

Make a well in the flour, pour in the milk and yeast mixture and mix until smooth and elastic, adding more milk if necessary to make a soft dough. Place the dough in a greased bowl, turning it over in the bowl so that it is lightly greased all over. Cover with a damp cloth and leave to rise in warm place for 45 to 50 minutes or until doubled in bulk. Knock down the dough, pull sides to centre, turn it over, then cover and allow to rise again for 30 minutes. Punch it down and roll out on a lightly floured board to 1 cm/½ inch thickness. Cut the dough into 8 strips, 2.5 cm/1 inch wide, and roll each into a rope 23 cm/9 inches long. Tie each rope into a loose knot with one end short. Pinch the short end to shape a head and beak, and press a clove in the head for an eye. Flatten the other end for the tail and snip the end 2 or 3 times for the feathers. Brush with lightly beaten egg and allow to rise. Bake in a preheated moderately hot oven (200°C/400°F, Gas Mark 6) for 15 minutes.

MAKES 8

Herb Soda Bread

METRIC/IMPERIAL	AMERICAN
25 g/1 oz mixed fresh herbs, leaves only (marjoram, parsley, chives, basil and rosemary) or 1 × 5 ml spoon/1 teaspoon dried mixed herbs	*1 oz mixed fresh herbs, leaves only (marjoram, parsley, chives, basil and rosemary) or 1 teaspoon dried mixed herbs*
100 g/4 oz wholewheat flour	*1 cup wholewheat flour*
100 g/4 oz plain flour, sifted	*1 cup all-purpose flour, sifted*
1 × 2.5 ml spoon/½ teaspoon bicarbonate of soda	*½ teaspoon baking soda*
1 × 2.5 ml spoon/½ teaspoon salt	*½ teaspoon salt*
50 g/2 oz butter, cut up into 4 pieces	*¼ cup butter, cut up into 4 pieces*
1 × 5 ml spoon/1 teaspoon cream of tartar	*1 teaspoon cream of tartar*
150 ml/¼ pint milk	*⅔ cup milk*
1 egg, beaten	*1 egg, beaten*
1 × 5 ml spoon/1 teaspoon caraway seeds	*1 teaspoon caraway seeds*

Chop the herbs and place in a bowl with the flours, soda and salt. Mix well. Add the butter and mix thoroughly. Stir the cream of tartar into the milk. Add to the bowl and blend until the mixture just forms a ball. Knead lightly on a floured surface into a round shape. Brush the top with the egg, and sprinkle over the caraway seeds. Cut into 4 pieces. Bake on a floured baking sheet in a moderately hot oven (200°C/400°F, Gas Mark 6) for about 25 minutes. Tap the bottom – if it sounds hollow it is cooked. Cool on a wire tray.

MAKES 4

Brazil Nut Loaf

METRIC/IMPERIAL	AMERICAN
225 g/8 oz shelled Brazil nuts	*2 cups shelled Brazil nuts*
100 g/4 oz wholewheat bread, cubed with crusts	*2 large slices wholewheat bread, cubed with crusts*
1 × 15 ml spoon/1 tablespoon oil	*1 tablespoon oil*
100 g/4 oz bacon, rinded and chopped	*6 slices bacon, rinded and chopped*
2 onions, peeled and chopped	*2 onions, peeled and chopped*
1 clove garlic, crushed	*1 clove garlic, crushed*
1 × 15 ml spoon/1 tablespoon chopped fresh parsley	*1 tablespoon chopped fresh parsley*
1 × 15 ml spoon/1 tablespoon chopped fresh thyme	*1 tablespoon chopped fresh thyme*
salt	*salt*
freshly ground black pepper	*freshly ground black pepper*
1 egg	*1 egg*
1 × 5 ml spoon/1 teaspoon Worcestershire sauce	*1 teaspoon Worcestershire sauce*

Put the nuts and bread in a blender or food processor and grind coarsely. Heat the oil in a pan, add the bacon, onions and garlic and fry gently for 4 to 5 minutes until soft. Remove the pan from the heat, then add the ground nut mixture, herbs and salt and pepper to taste. Mix well. Beat the egg with the Worcestershire sauce, add to the nut mixture and bind thoroughly. Press the mixture into a lightly greased 450 g/1 lb loaf tin (7 × 3 inch loaf pan) and level the surface. Bake in a preheated moderately hot oven (190°C/375°F, Gas Mark 5) for 40 minutes until the top is crisp and lightly browned. Invert the loaf out on to a serving dish and serve hot. Alternatively leave to cool in the tin (pan), then invert and serve cold with sliced tomatoes.

SERVES 4 TO 6

Cardamom Braid

METRIC/IMPERIAL	AMERICAN
For the dough:	For the dough:
1–2 × 5 ml spoons/1–2 teaspoons ground cardamom	*1–2-teaspoons ground cardamom*
250 g/9 oz plain flour	*2¼ cups all-purpose flour*
pinch salt	*pinch salt*
25–120 ml/1–4 fl oz milk	*2 tablespoons–1 cup milk*
50 g/2 oz butter	*¼ cup butter*
15 g/½ oz fresh yeast	*½ cake compressed yeast*
50 g/2 oz caster sugar	*¼ cup sugar*
1 egg, beaten	*1 egg, beaten*
For the glaze:	For the glaze:
1 egg	*1 egg*
2 × 5 ml spoons/2 teaspoons milk	*2 teaspoons milk*
caster sugar	*sugar*

Add ground cardamom to the flour. Sift the flour with salt into a bowl. Heat 50 ml/2 fl oz (¼ cup) of milk to lukewarm, add butter and allow to melt. Add to the yeast and stir until dissolved. Mix in the sugar and beaten egg. Make a well in the flour, pour in the milk mixture and stir until smooth, first with a wooden spoon and then with the hand. Add more warm milk if necessary to make a soft dough. When the dough comes away cleanly from the sides of the bowl, turn on to a floured surface and knead until smooth and elastic. Add a little more flour if the dough is too soft to knead.

Place the dough in a greased bowl, turning it over in the bowl so that it is lightly greased all over. Cover with a damp cloth and leave to rise in a warm place for 45 to 50 minutes or until doubled in bulk.

Turn on to a floured surface and knead lightly. Divide into three equal portions and shape each piece into a rope about 1 cm/½ inch in diameter. Line the ropes up together on a greased baking sheet and, starting from the middle, plait loosely towards the ends, taking care not to stretch the dough. Seal the ends by pinching well together. Cover and leave in a warm place to rise until doubled in bulk. Beat the egg and milk and brush over the braid. Spinkle generously with some sugar and bake in a preheated moderate oven (180°C/350°F, Gas Mark 4) for 30 to 35 minutes, or until brown. Remove to a wire rack and cover loosely with a tea (dish) towel. Cool before slicing.

Brazil Nut Loaf

Hot Cheese and Anchovy Bread

METRIC/IMPERIAL
1 loaf crusty Italian bread
4 × 15 ml spoons/4 tablespoons olive oil
75 g/3 oz butter, softened
1 clove garlic, crushed
1 small can flat anchovy fillets, drained
100 g/4 oz Mozzarella or Provolone cheese, cut up into shreds
2 × 15 ml spoons/2 tablespoons capers, drained and chopped

AMERICAN
1 loaf crusty Italian bread
¼ cup olive oil
⅓ cup butter, softened
1 clove garlic, crushed
1 small can flat anchovy fillets, drained
¼ lb Mozzarella or Provolone cheese, cut up into shreds
2 tablespoons capers, drained and chopped

Slice the loaf in half lengthwise. Combine the olive oil, butter, garlic and anchovies in a small bowl, mashing to a smooth paste. Spread on both halves of bread, and sprinkle one half with cheese and capers. Join the halves together and wrap tightly in aluminium foil. Heat on a barbecue for 5 minutes or in a preheated very hot oven (240°C/475°F, Gas Mark 9) for 10 minutes.
SERVES 4 TO 6

Garlic Bread with Herbs

METRIC/IMPERIAL
75 g/3 oz butter, softened
2–4 cloves garlic, crushed
2–4 × 5 ml spoons/2–4 teaspoons chopped fresh herbs or 1–2 × 5 ml spoons/1–2 teaspoons dried mixed herbs
1 loaf French bread

AMERICAN
⅓ cup butter, softened
2–4 cloves garlic, crushed
2–4 teaspoons chopped fresh herbs or 1–2 × 5 teaspoons dried mixed herbs
1 loaf French bread

Beat the butter with a wooden spoon, gradually beating in the garlic and herbs. Slice the loaf, making sure not to cut right through to the base of the loaf and spread each slice with a little flavoured butter. Wrap tightly in aluminium foil and, if possible, allow to stand for 1 hour or so before baking. Bake in a preheated moderately hot oven (200°C/400°F, Gas Mark 6) for 10 to 15 minutes. Serve hot or cold with appetizers or soups.
SERVES 4 TO 6

Preserves

Spiced Apple and Rum Conserve

METRIC/IMPERIAL

1 kg/2 lb cooking apples, roughly cut up
1.2 litres/2 pints water
25 g/1 oz root ginger, peeled and chopped
grated rind and juice 2 lemons
approx 1.25 kg/$2\frac{3}{4}$ lb sugar
225 g/8 oz sultanas
1 kg/2 lb dessert apples
6 × 15 ml spoons/6 tablespoons rum (optional)

AMERICAN

2 lb tart apples, roughly cut up
5 cups water
1 oz ginger root, peeled and chopped
grated rind and juice 2 lemons
approx $2\frac{3}{4}$ lb sugar
$1\frac{1}{3}$ cups golden raisins
2 lb dessert apples
6 tablespoons rum (optional)

Place the cooking apples in a pan with the water, ginger and lemon rind. Cover the pan and bring to the boil. Reduce the heat and simmer for about 1 hour or until the apples are very soft. Rub the apple mixture through a sieve (strainer) with a wooden spoon. Add the lemon juice to the apple purée, then measure and add 450 g/1 lb/2 cups sugar for every 600 ml/1 pint/$2\frac{1}{2}$ cups purée. Transfer the purée and sugar to a large pan and add the sultanas (golden raisins). Heat gently, stirring until the sugar is dissolved, then bring to the boil. Reduce the heat and simmer for 5 minutes. Cut the dessert apples into quarters, core (peel if liked) and cut into thin slices. Add the apple slices to the pan and cook gently for 15 minutes or until the apple slices are tender but still retain their shape. Stir in the rum, if used, and cool completely before pouring into prepared jars. Cover with a small waxed disc (waxed side down) and press gently to exclude the air. Cover the jars with cellophane and secure with a rubber band or string. Clean and label the jars with the date and type of jam.
MAKES ABOUT 3 kg/7 lb

Cidered Apple Cheese (Butter)

METRIC/IMPERIAL

1.75 kg/4 lb cooking apples, chopped
1.2 litres/2 pints cider
1 stick cinnamon
1 × 5 ml spoon/1 teaspoon whole cloves
approx 1.5 kg/3 lb granulated or brown sugar

AMERICAN

4 lb tart apples, chopped
$2\frac{1}{2}$ cups apple cider
1 stick cinnamon
1 teaspoon whole cloves
6 cups granulated or 7 cups brown sugar

Place the apples in a saucepan with the cider and spices. Cover and cook gently, stirring occasionally, for about 20 minutes or until soft and pulpy. Rub through a sieve (strainer) and weigh the purée. Add 350 g/12 oz/$1\frac{1}{2}$–2 cups sugar for every 450 g/1 lb purée. Return the purée with the sugar to a clean saucepan. Stir over a gentle heat until the sugar dissolves. Continue to cook for about 20 minutes, stirring occasionally, until it is a thick creamy consistency. Pour into prepared oiled jars, and cover with a waxed disc and cellophane as for Spiced Apples and Rum Conserve and label. Keeps for 3 to 6 months.
MAKES ABOUT 2.25/5 lb

Mint Jelly

METRIC/IMPERIAL

1.5 kg/3 lb cooking apples
1.2 litres/2 pints water
600 ml/1 pint wine vinegar
bunch of fresh mint
approx 750 g/$1\frac{1}{2}$ lb sugar
few drops green food colouring (optional)

AMERICAN

3 lb cooking apples
5 cups water
$2\frac{1}{2}$ cups wine vinegar
bunch of fresh mint
approx $1\frac{1}{2}$ lb sugar
few drops green food colouring (optional)

Wash the apples, cut up into pieces and place in a large pan. Pour over the water and vinegar. Strip off the best leaves from the mint and reserve to make about 3 to 4 tablespoons chopped mint. Add the remaining mint, with stalks, to the pan. Bring to the boil and simmer gently for about 45 minutes or until the apples are very soft.

Strain through a jelly bag and leave to drip for at least 2 hours or overnight. Measure the juice, pour into a large pan and bring to the boil. Add 450 g/1 lb sugar for every 600 ml/1 pint/$2\frac{1}{2}$ cups juice. Heat gently, stirring until the sugar is dissolved. Bring to the boil, then boil rapidly until setting point is reached. Remove any scum immediately and stir in the reserved chopped mint. Cool slightly until a thin skin forms on the surface, stir gently and pour into prepared jars. Cover and label.
MAKES ABOUT $1\frac{1}{2}$ kg/3 lb

Variations:
Other fresh herbs can be substituted for mint, e.g. thyme, sage, parsley and rosemary. Serve with roast meats – rosemary jelly with lamb, thyme jelly with poultry, sage jelly with pork and parsley jelly with cold gammon.

Tomato and Herb Jelly; Mint Jelly

Tomato and Herb Jelly

METRIC/IMPERIAL
1.5 kg/3 lb tomatoes
300 ml/½ pint water
300 ml/½ pint vinegar
2 lemons, sliced
bunch of fresh herbs (rosemary, thyme, mint, parsley, bay leaf)
approx 1 kg/2 lb sugar

AMERICAN
3 lb tomatoes
1¼ cups water
1¼ cups vinegar
2 lemons, sliced
bunch of fresh herbs (rosemary, thyme, mint, parsley, bay leaf)
approx 2 lb sugar

Wash the tomatoes, cut into quarters and place in a large pan. Pour over the water and vinegar and add the lemons. Add the herbs, about 12 sprigs altogether (use just one herb or a mixture of herbs as desired). Bring to the boil and simmer gently for about 30 minutes or until the tomatoes are very soft. Strain through a jelly bag and leave to drip for at least 2 hours or overnight.

Measure the juice, pour into a large pan and bring to the boil. Add 500 g/1 lb sugar for every 600 ml/1 pint/2½ cups juice. Heat gently, stirring until the sugar is dissolved. Bring to the boil, then boil rapidly until setting point is reached. Remove any scum immediately and pour into prepared jars. (If liked, place a sprig of fresh herbs in the jar before pouring in the jelly to vary the flavour and appearance.) Cover and label. Serve with meat, especially lamb. Half the quantity of tomatoes may be replaced with chopped cooking apples.

MAKES ABOUT 1½ kg/3 lb

Queen of Jams

METRIC/IMPERIAL	AMERICAN
1.5 kg/3 lb peaches	*3 lb peaches*
grated rind and juice 4 large lemons, pith and pips reserved	*grated rind and juice 4 large lemons, pith and seeds reserved*
450 ml/¾ pint water	*2 cups water*
1 stick cinnamon	*1 stick cinnamon*
1 × 2.5 ml spoon/½ teaspoon whole cloves	*½ teaspoon whole cloves*
1 × 2.5 ml spoon/½ teaspoon allspice berries	*½ teaspoon allspice berries*
1.5 kg/3 lb preserving sugar	*3 lb preserving sugar*

Skin the peaches by steeping in boiling water for 10 to 20 seconds; drain and skin them. Cut in half, through to the stone (pit), twist to separate the 2 halves and remove the stones (pits). Slice the peaches and place in a large pan. Crack open the peach stones (pits) with a hammer, remove the skins from the kernels, then add kernels to the peaches. Add grated rind and juice of the lemons and pour over the water.

Tie the peach stones (pits), lemon pith and pips (seeds), and spices in a muslin (cheesecloth) bag and add to the pan. Heat gently and simmer for about 30 minutes or until the peaches are soft but still retain their shape. Remove the muslin (cheesecloth) bag, squeezing the juice back into the pan. Add the sugar and heat gently, stirring until the sugar is dissolved. Bring to the boil, then boil rapidly until setting point is reached. Remove the scum. Cool slightly, stir, then pour into prepared jars. Cover and label as for Spiced Apple and Rum Conserve.

MAKES ABOUT 2.75 kg/6 lb

Spiced Apple Jelly

METRIC/IMPERIAL	AMERICAN
2 kg/4½ lb cooking or crab apples	*4½ lb tart or crab apples*
1.75 litres/3 pints water	*7½ cups water*
2 lemons, sliced	*2 lemons, sliced*
25 g/1 oz root ginger, finely chopped or bruised	*1 oz ginger root, finely chopped or bruised*
1 stick cinnamon	*1 stick cinnamon*
1 × 2.5 ml spoon/½ teaspoon whole cloves	*½ teaspoon whole cloves*
approx 750 g/1½ lb sugar	*approx 3 cups sugar*

A few red berries may be added to the apples to give an attractive pale rose-coloured jelly. Rose geranium leaves or lemon balm leaves may be added for extra flavour, and cider substituted for some of the water.

Wash the apples, cut up into pieces, discarding any bad bits, and place in a large pan. Pour over the water and add the lemons and spices. Bring to the boil and simmer gently for 45 minutes to 1 hour or until the apples are very soft. Strain through a jelly bag and leave to drip for at least 2 hours or overnight. Measure the juice, pour into a large saucepan and bring to the boil. Add 450 g/1 lb (2 cups) sugar for every 600 ml/1 pint/2½ cups juice. Heat gently, stirring until the sugar is dissolved. Bring to the boil, then boil rapidly until setting point is reached. Remove the scum immediately and pour into prepared jars. Cover and label as for Spiced Apple and Rum Conserve.

MAKES ABOUT 1.5 kg/3 lb

Spiced Redcurrant Jelly

METRIC/IMPERIAL	AMERICAN
1.75 kg/4 lb redcurrants	*4 lb red currants*
1.2 litres/2 pints water	*5 cups water*
1 × 5 ml spoon/1 teaspoon allspice berries	*1 teaspoon allspice berries*
1 × 2.5 ml spoon/½ teaspoon whole cloves	*½ teaspoon whole cloves*
2 large blades mace	*2 large blades mace*
1 stick cinnamon	*1 stick cinnamon*
approx 450 g/1 lb sugar	*2 cups sugar*

Rinse the redcurrants and place in a large pan. Pour over the water and add the spices. Bring to the boil and simmer gently for about 40 minutes or until very soft, crushing the redcurrants occasionally. Strain through a jelly bag, and leave to drip for at least 2 hours or overnight. Measure the juice, pour into a large pan and bring to the boil. Add 450 g/1 lb sugar for every 600 ml/1 pint/2½ cups juice. Heat gently, stirring until the sugar is dissolved. Bring to the boil, then boil rapidly until setting point is reached. Remove the scum immediately and pour into prepared jars. Cover and label as for Spiced Apple and Rum Conserve.

MAKES ABOUT 1 kg/2 lb

Orange and Thyme Jelly

METRIC/IMPERIAL	AMERICAN
1 kg/2 lb oranges	*2 lb oranges*
1 kg/2 lb lemons	*2 lb lemons*
2 litres/3½ pints water	*9 cups water*
approx 750 g/1½ lb sugar	*approx 3 cups sugar*
4 × 15 ml spoons/4 tablespoons fresh thyme	*4 tablespoons fresh thyme*

Wash the oranges and lemons and cut up into small pieces (slice, then cut the slices into halves or quarters). Place the orange and lemon pieces in a large pan and pour over the water. Bring to the boil and simmer for about 1 hour or until the fruit is soft. Strain through a jelly bag and leave to drip for at least 2 hours or overnight. Measure the juice, pour into a large pan and bring to the boil. Add 450 g/1 lb sugar for every 600 ml/1 pint/2½ cups juice. Heat gently, stirring until the sugar is dissolved. Bring to the boil, then boil rapidly until setting point is reached. Remove any scum immediately and stir in the thyme. Cool slightly until a thin skin forms on the surface, stir gently and pour into prepared jars. Cover and label as for Spiced Apple and Rum Conserve.

MAKES ABOUT 1.5 kg/3 lb

Orange and Thyme Jelly

Drinks

Spiced Blackberry Cordial

METRIC/IMPERIAL
1¾ kg/4 lb blackberries
600 ml/1 pint water
1 × 15 ml spoon/1 tablespoon whole cloves
1 × 15 ml spoon/1 tablespoon grated nutmeg
2 sticks cinnamon
approx 450 g/1 lb sugar
300 ml/½ pint brandy

AMERICAN
4 lb blackberries
2½ cups water
1 tablespoon whole cloves
1 tablespoon grated nutmeg
2 sticks cinnamon
approx 2 cups sugar
1¼ cups brandy

Place the blackberries in a pan with the water and spices. Cover and bring to the boil. Reduce the heat, then simmer for 15 minutes or until the blackberries are soft. Strain through a sieve (strainer) or muslin (cheesecloth) and measure the juice. For every 600 ml/1 pint/2½ cups juice, add 450 g/1 lb/2 cups sugar and stir until dissolved. If necessary, heat gently to dissolve the sugar, then stir in the brandy. Pour into prepared bottles, straining to remove seeds if necessary.
MAKES ABOUT 1.75 LITRES/3 PINTS/7½ CUPS

Mint Julep

METRIC/IMPERIAL
16–20 sprigs young mint
2 × 15 ml spoons/2 tablespoons sugar
2 × 15 ml spoons/2 tablespoons water
crushed ice
icing sugar (optional)
2 double measures brandy, whisky, gin or bourbon (and a dash of rum if brandy used)
fresh fruit in season

AMERICAN
16–20 sprigs young mint
2 tablespoons sugar
2 tablespoons water
crushed ice
confectioners' sugar (optional)
2 double measures brandy, whisky, gin or bourbon (and dash of rum if brandy used)
fresh fruit in season

Crush half the mint and the sugar with a spoon until the sugar dissolves. Add the water and mix until all the mint flavour is extracted. Take a tumbler or a large balloon wine glass, almost fill with crushed ice and push remaining mint in, stalks downwards. If liked, dip the leaves first in icing (confectioners') sugar. Strain the prepared mint mixture into the glass and pour in the spirit. Decorate the top of the ice with small pieces of fruit in season, choosing the most colourful available. Put in a couple of drinking straws and serve. If using brandy, add just a dash of rum on top.
SERVES 2

Spiced Blackberry Cordial

Minted Iced Tea

METRIC/IMPERIAL

1 lemon, finely chopped
1 × 15 ml spoon/1 tablespoon sugar
8 fresh sprigs mint
1.2 litres/2 pints weak tea, strained
4–8 halved lemon slices to garnish

AMERICAN

1 lemon, finely chopped
1 tablespoon sugar
8 fresh sprigs mint
5 cups weak tea, strained
4–8 halved lemon slices to garnish

Put the chopped lemon in the bottom of a jug with the sugar and 4 of the mint sprigs, chopped. Pour on the tea. Allow the mixture to infuse for 20 to 30 minutes, then strain into a suitable container. Chill well. To serve, decorate each glass with a sprig of mint and a halved lemon slice.
SERVES 4 TO 8

Herb and Lemon Tea

METRIC/IMPERIAL

1 × 15 ml spoon/1 tablespoon coarsely chopped fresh herbs (mint, rosemary, thyme)
finely grated rind and juice $\frac{1}{2}$ small lemon
600 ml/1 pint boiling water

AMERICAN

1 tablespoon coarsely chopped fresh herbs (mint, rosemary, thyme)
finely grated rind and juice $\frac{1}{2}$ small lemon
$2\frac{1}{2}$ cups boiling water

Put the herbs, lemon rind and juice in a bowl. Pour over the boiling water, cover and leave to infuse for 3 to 5 minutes. Strain into cups and serve hot.
MAKES 600 ml/1 PINT/$2\frac{1}{2}$ CUPS

Coconut Milk

METRIC/IMPERIAL

350 ml/12 fl oz milk
1 × 5 ml spoon/1 teaspoon ground coriander
$\frac{1}{2}$ × 5 ml spoon/$\frac{1}{2}$ teaspoon ground cumin
115 g/$4\frac{1}{2}$ oz desiccated coconut

AMERICAN

$1\frac{1}{2}$ cups milk
1 teaspoon ground coriander
$\frac{1}{2}$ teaspoon ground cumin
$1\frac{1}{2}$ cups shredded coconut

Heat the milk with the coriander and cumin, add the coconut and bring slowly to the boil. Allow to cool slightly. Put into a blender or food processor at high speed for 2 to 3 minutes. Pour into a sieve (strainer) and knead the coconut well to extract all the milk. This is the first extract or thick milk sometimes known as coconut cream. Repeat the process with the same coconut and 350 ml/12 fl oz/$1\frac{1}{2}$ cups fresh milk; this gives a thinner milk, with a good flavour and can be used in curries or served as a flavoured milk.

Spiced Mulled Cider

METRIC/IMPERIAL

2 × 15 ml spoons/2 tablespoons soft brown sugar
pinch salt
2.25 litres/4 pints dry cider
1 × 5 ml spoon/1 teaspoon allspice berries
large pinch grated nutmeg
5 cm/2 inch stick cinnamon
1 orange

AMERICAN

2 tablespoons light brown sugar
pinch salt
5 pints apple cider
1 teaspoon allspice berries
large pinch grated nutmeg
2 inch stick cinnamon
1 orange

Mix the brown sugar, salt and cider together in a saucepan. Place the allspice and nutmeg in a square of muslin (cheesecloth), tie into a small package and add to the cider with the cinnamon stick. Bring slowly to just under boiling point. Add twists of orange rind and a slice of orange when serving.
SERVES 8 TO 10

Guy Fawkes' Punch

METRIC/IMPERIAL

2 × 15 ml spoons/2 tablespoons brandy
1 × 411 g/$14\frac{1}{2}$ oz can apricot slices
1 litre red wine
2 × 15 ml spoons/2 tablespoons dry sherry
3 × 15 ml spoons/3 tablespoons port
300 ml/$\frac{1}{2}$ pint water
1 cinnamon stick
12 cloves

AMERICAN

2 tablespoons brandy
1 can (16 oz) apricot slices
4 cups red wine
2 tablespoons dry sherry
3 tablespoons port
$1\frac{1}{4}$ cups water
1 cinnamon stick
12 cloves

Mix together the brandy and apricot slices, with their juice. Put the wine, sherry, port, water, cinnamon and cloves in a saucepan and bring slowly to the boil. Add the fruit mixture and serve hot.
SERVES 8

Lemonade

METRIC/IMPERIAL

250 g/8 oz sugar
600 ml/1 pint water
2 × 15 ml spoons/2 tablespoons lemon juice per glass
ice cubes
soda water or water
fresh mint sprigs
lemon slices

AMERICAN

$\frac{1}{2}$ lb sugar
$2\frac{1}{2}$ cups water
2 tablespoons lemon juice per glass
ice cubes
soda water or water
fresh mint sprigs
lemon slices

Put the sugar and water in a saucepan and stir to dissolve over a low heat. Allow to cool and use this as a base for lemonade drinks. Place 3 to 4 tablespoons of the sugar syrup in a tall glass with the lemon juice. Add ice cubes and fill the glass with soda water, or water if a still drink is preferred. Decorate with a sprig of mint and a slice of lemon.

Lemonade; Spiced Mulled Cider; Guy Fawkes' Punch

Glossary

Basil: Often used in Italian cooking, especially with tomatoes, pasta, eggs and mushrooms. Also good in salad and salad dressings, and added to melted butter sauce for grilled (broiled) fish.

Bay: Use leaves fresh or dried in *bouquets garnis*. Add to marinades, stews, stocks and soups and to water when poaching fish. Infuse a leaf in milk then strain out before making a white sauce.

Caraway: The seeds are used in cakes, biscuits and buns and also in pork and liver dishes, cabbage, cauliflower and potatoes.

Chervil: Use the leaves chopped as a garnish for meat dishes or vegetables such as carrots, tomatoes and peas, and also in mixtures of chopped herbs in omelettes or cheese dishes.

Chives: Use chopped chives as a garnish on salads, cold soups and vegetable dishes. Add them to omelettes or mix with soured cream and serve with baked potatoes.

Cinnamon: Use stick cinnamon in spicy meat dishes (remove the stick before serving) and to make spiced drinks such as mulled wine. Use the ground spice in baking, and with stewed fruit.

Cloves: Stick 2 or 3 cloves in an onion and add to the pan when making stock, or infuse in milk before making bread sauce. Add cloves to mulled wine, or stewed fruit.

Coriander: Use the leaves to garnish and flavour Middle Eastern and Indian meat dishes. Use the seeds whole with vegetables or in pickles and chutneys, or ground as part of curry spice mixtures, or in baking spiced cakes and buns.

Cumin: Add the seed to meat dishes and to dishes made from dried beans and pulses. Sprinkle the seeds over savoury rice just before serving and mix into mashed potatoes. Use ground seed for spiced cakes and biscuits.

Dill: Add finely chopped leaves to cucumber salad, or add to salad dressings. Add to sauces for fish and use whole leaves for garnish. Use whole or ground dill seed in herb butters, bean soups, lamb stews and for pickling cucumbers.

Fennel: Add fennel seeds or leaves to the water for poaching fish or chop the leaves into sauces for fish. Use seeds to flavour breads and savoury biscuits (crackers). Chopped leaves can be used as a garnish for cooked or raw vegetables.

Ginger: Grate fresh root ginger and use for curries and other meat dishes. Use powdered ginger in baking and for fruit desserts.

Juniper: Crush dried berries and add to marinades for pork and game. Use in stuffings for goose and duck. Add a few berries to the water when cooking cabbage or boiling ham.

Mace: Infuse a blade in milk before making white sauce, cheese soufflé or bread sauce. Use powdered mace in mushroom dishes or in baking spiced cakes and buns.

Marjoram: Use fresh sweet marjoram in meat loaf and with vegetable dishes such as potatoes and marrow (squash) or courgettes (zucchini). Use dried wild marjoram (oregano) in Italian dishes such as pizzas and pasta dishes.

Mint: Chop leaves and use as a garnish for salads and vegetable dishes. Stir chopped leaves into yogurt as a dressing for cucumber salad. Add a sprig to cooking water when boiling new potatoes or peas. Serve mint sauce with lamb.

Nutmeg: Grate into white sauces, cheese sauces and egg dishes, also spiced drinks, biscuits and buns.

Parsley: Add finely chopped leaves generously to salads, vegetable dishes, rice, soups, meat and fish dishes. Make parsley butter to serve with steaks, chops and grilled fish. Deep fry small sprigs and serve with fried fish.

Rosemary: Scatter rosemary over lamb before roasting, or add to other meat dishes, or fish such as halibut. Small sprigs can be added to wine and fruit cups or to fruit salad.

Sage: Used with roast pork (particularly as sage and onion stuffing), also with duck or in meat stews. Add chopped leaves sparingly to salads, tomatoes, cream cheese spreads and in stuffed onions.

Tarragon: Excellent in sauces to serve with fish, meat or vegetables and goes particularly well with fish and poultry. Chopped leaves are good in salads and salad dressings. Steep a sprig in a bottle of wine vinegar to make tarragon vinegar.

Thyme: An essential ingredient of *bouquet garni*, sprigs can also be added to any meat or raw vegetable stew, or stock or soup. Use in stuffings or chop the leaves very finely over vegetables.

Acknowledgements

The publishers wish to thank the following for their permission to reproduce the photographs in this book:

Bryce Attwell 2–3, 4–5, 93, Rex Bamber 69, Bob Golden 6, 9, 46, 65, 72–73, Melvin Grey 1 & 23, 17, 24–25, 27, 31, 49, 53, 55, 56, 81, 87, 88–89, Gina Harris 11, 12, 13, 14, 16, 20, 21, 28, 29, 34, 39, 41, 50, 62–63, 70, 77, 78, 83, Paul Kemp 45, Norman Nicholls 19, 33, 43, 59, Roger Phillips 60, 67, 75, 84–85, 90–91.

Index